My First Life

My First Life
By Henry Goldsmith

authorHOUSE®

Henry Gold Smith's post card
from Amsterdam to
Gisela Samuel 1941

Henry Gold Smith in Aspen,
Colorado 1988

AuthorHouse™
1663 Liberty Drive
Bloomington, IN 47403
www.authorhouse.com
Phone: 1-800-839-8640

First published by AuthorHouse   09/22/2011

ISBN: 978-1-4670-3626-9 (sc)
ISBN: 978-1-4670-3625-2 (ebk)

Library of Congress Control Number: 2011916518

Printed in the United States of America

CONTENTS

A Note of Thanks . . .

THIS BOOK WOULD not have been possible without the patience and cooperation of my wife, Ellen, who made an all-out attempt to shelter me in my working area during some long winter nights.

I also acknowledge the clerical expertise of Ita and Lorraine, who kept me away from the typewriter.

—Henry L. Goldsmith

FOREWORD

HENRY GOLDSMITH LIVED the American Dream as well and as successfully as anyone can who was born in another place in a very different time. He arrived in New York with his wife and infant son, Frank after World War II and by 1954 owned a house and an electronics business in Queens, New York. He was the father of two sons and, eventually, the grandfather of two more. In the 1950s he became passionate about skiing; the 1970s he bought a summer house north of the city, the better to indulge in it. The skiing resolved him to move to Aspen, Colorado, in 1975, where he started another electronics store. He retired in 1986 without ever having slowed down much. He worked out at the Aspen Athletic Club, went to the mountains whenever he could, and took up volunteer work, giving talks at local schools about his first life, the one that ended when he came to America, and the one you will read about here.

As to what kind of man he was, the measure of his character, the impact he made on the different times he lived, his family knows, as do his friends, as will the people who read this book. Words that will likely come to mind include energetic, determined, and quick thinking. American virtues, all of them. Virtues that grow in this country but don't have to be native to it. Perhaps he could be more ruthless than most people know how to be—but the world, by the time he reached the New one, had handed him reasons to develop that trait. Wherever he found himself, he never did worse than survive—itself too often a huge task—and when circumstances allowed, he turned his gifts toward prospering. This book, really, is less about all of that than about how he survived twelve years on a continent ruled by the Nazis, who were determined to murder him for being a Jew.

When Henry died in 2001, he left behind a manuscript about how he survived the Holocaust to enter what he always referred to as his second life. As to his first life . . . Six million dead, and we don't know what stories those individuals would tell from wherever they have gone. That's six million stories, gone. Those six million have one single story to tell the world, which in itself is a form of immolation—to condense six million individual lives to one number, one story. About what those individuals experienced, we only know what the survivors can tell us about it, and there are plenty of memoirs to enlighten us on that, all of them important for their testimony, but—just as important—for the reminder they offer that everyone who was murdered in the camps or the eastern forests was an individual who today must rely on others' memories to speak for them.

There is a question that serves as an undertow to all Holocaust memoirs: How did these ones survive? There are different ways to look at it. Some survived by losing their moral compass, or by never having had one. Henry was not one of those—but they were out there, the *kapos*, the ghetto police, the ones who helped the Nazis do their work in exchange for a little more time. Some were simply fortunate, the recipients of one or more random acts of chance that fell in their favor, acts as simple as a wave of a riding crop on a railroad siding or a work detail that turned toward the camp gates. Some of them escaped the Third Reich overseas, and some were hidden by those good people on both sides whom any war seems too busy to interfere with. And then some were fortunate, but something inside them provided more than luck, or made them know how to use the luck that opened for them. And some, finally, became fighters of some kind. They might not have become that otherwise, but the war brought out that side of them. Henry was one of them, and let us not forget how many were like him. Whether they were fighting a partisan war in the Russian forests, or going underground in Western Europe, they survived by learning to strike back at a world that had struck first.

And that last way, really, brings us to Henry's story. Staying alive can be one way of fighting back, but it is possible to do more, and Henry was one who did. He survived by fleeing to Holland, and from there finding a way to join the French Resistance. And when the Nazis found him anyway . . . well, read on. I'm sure you'll have read nothing like it before.

Every manuscript has its own story besides the one it contains. In 1998, an American named Joe Rosenbaum attended a Rotary Club meeting in Aspen, Colorado, and found himself seated next to an older gentleman, a Holocaust survivor with a German accent named Kurt

Bresnitz. They got to talking, and Joe learned that Kurt had escaped Nazi-occupied Europe from his birthplace, Vienna. And Kurt, it turned out, had a friend in Aspen named Henry, who had written a wonderful book about his own struggles against the Nazi regime. He had written the manuscript in English, which was not his native tongue, and Kurt described how Henry was struggling to get his story published. The wheels in Joe's head began to turn. He had just returned with his wife from a visit to Auschwitz, on the March of the Living and he was of a mind to do something about what he seen there.

Joe gave Henry a call, and they got along well, but Henry died before they could meet. But Henry have sons Frank and Steven who was anxious for his father's story to be published they gave Joe a copy of the manuscript. From that day on, Joe made it a cause to find a publisher for *My First Life*. He recruited his son-in-law, Ben Hunter, for help, and Ben after a series of side alleys found his way to an editor in Toronto, Matthew Kudelka, who makes one specialty of stories like Henry's.

All of the people mentioned in this foreword hope that the story you're about to read is as amazing to you as it has been to us.

Henry wasn't a professional writer, and his English, while good, was not his first language. His story has not been altered in any way, nor has anything been deleted or added. But if he would have said something in a different way if his English had been stronger, he has been helped.

Finally, we can wish he had been here to add to his account, because the book would have been longer and perhaps richer, and there are some inevitable lacunae. Gaps that relate to the historical record have been filled with a word or two. But there are others that only he could have filled for us. How did he actually join the French Resistance? We'll never know. What happened to the other people in the book? His family, his friends, his lovers. Henry Goldsmith died May 3, 2001, his wife Ellen died Dec 23,2010, Gilsela Samrels Sichrer Lives is Israel.

His son Frank and wife Cynthia and two sons Alex and Garrett live in Aspen CO, Steven Frank's younger brother lives in Hawaii. It's too late to ask Henry. So we ask you to tolerate that. He was not a professional writer, which besides drawbacks, has its advantages. Mainly, the advantage of authenticity, because you will know that he was there, and that this is what he saw and did.

—Matthew Kudelka 2009/2011

1

ESSEN, GERMANY

THE YEAR WAS 1921. Germany had lost its war two-and-a-half years earlier. The country was in turmoil and inflation was soaring to unimaginable levels. The U.S. dollar had been worth 35 marks the year before. Now it was worth 184, and by 1923 it would be worth 4.2 *billion*. In those days, it was fashionable to light your cigar using a million-mark note for a taper.

For a time after the war ended in 1918, radical political parties from the right and the left had conducted pitched battles on the streets of German cities, both sides trying to undermine the postwar government of Friedrich Ebert. The far-left Spartacist League had made an especially strong show, under the leadership of Karl Liebknecht and Rosa Luxemburg. In 1919, after those two were murdered by the Freikorps, far-right paramilitaries, the Spartacists renamed themselves the German Communist Party (KPD). The country was only beginning to calm down.

The Treaty of Versailles had crushed and humiliated Germany. The victors had demanded, and received, huge reparation payments from Germany as punishment for starting the war. The loser also had to give back certain border territories to their original owners. Meanwhile, Allied soldiers continued to occupy parts of the Rhineland and the Ruhr. The bitterness on both sides was palpable.

In June 1922, Walter Rathenau, Germany's Secretary for Reconstruction, was assassinated by two right-wing army officers. In November of the following year, in Munich, a cashiered army corporal and political firebrand named Adolf Hitler attempted to launch a revolution in the name of National Socialism. He failed miserably, but fourteen people died during the attempt and Hitler was sentenced to five years' imprisonment in Landsberg Castle (he was released after nine months). He passed his days in prison dictating *Mein Kampf* to his cellmate, Rudolph Hess. The people of Germany were looking for people to blame for the lost war, and they soon began turning out in droves to listen to Hitler, who was a mesmerizing speaker with a clear political message.

By then, Alfred Goldschmitt was thirty-nine years old and had been married for one year to Sabine, whom he had met when she was a saleswoman at the Freudenberg Department Store. Alfred was a widower, his first wife having died of an incurable illness, leaving him with two daughters, Friedel and Irma, twelve and ten years old.

A proud veteran of the Great War, he married Sabine despite some misgivings. She was a devout Jew, the daughter of a large, conservative family in the central Rhine, and he was not. "Which way should I turn?" he wondered. Should he continue to be a German patriot or should he embrace Judaism? By then, Theodor Herzl had scandalized many people with his insistence that Judaism had to become more than a religion—it must become a political entity with its own state.

Alfred was an decent and honorable man, the owner of a tobacco shop, who took an active part in community affairs, but when it came to religion, he had his own creed: "Act according to your conscience and don't be afraid of anybody."

It wasn't easy for him to support his family during the economic turmoil that bedeviled postwar Germany, but he had ambition, a keen eye for business, and the help of a good woman both in the shop and at home. So he succeeded.

On March 14, 1923, I entered this world. I was the first son in the family, and the first and most probably the only child of Alfred's new marriage, with two babysitters ready and waiting for me. I was loved at first sight by everyone, without even having to ask.

I was nicknamed Heinz, and would be called "Heinzchen" for many years. To honor my grandfather, they gave me the middle name of Leo.

There was no longer open war on the streets, but Germany still faced enormous problems, including an unstable government. In 1925, General Paul von Hindenburg was elected president at the age of 78. He was an aristocrat as well as war hero. Unfortunately he was head of state only in name, and while the political turmoil continued, unemployment continued to soar.

My parents dealt with a very popular product that most people used, so they were able to open two more stores in different parts of the city, which at the time had a population of around 650,000. We rented an apartment behind the original store. Even in those days security was an issue, so my parents bought a full-grown German Shepherd and trained him to protect both the shop and our home. Rolf was so aggressive and powerful that one day he killed a smaller dog while playing with it. My parents had to build a cage for him in our backyard. Only at night did they give him free run, attached to a long chain.

Rolf let me get away with everything, and the rougher I played, the better he liked it. But as it turned out, he had his limits. One day when I was four, I discovered the miracle of a yardstick and spent a whole afternoon pretending to measure everything around me. Running out of objects, I turned my attention to my four-legged Rolf. Such a beautiful long muzzle he had. I placed my yardstick on top of it. That he considered an aggressive act, and he retaliated by snapping at my lower lip and taking a little chunk out of it. The scar remains to this day. Such was my first encounter with danger.

I grew old enough to have my own bedroom, small but mine. I'm not quite sure whether the framed poem by Goethe over my bed was meant to be an inspiration or just a decoration. I must have decided quite early it was the former. Those lines read: "Allen Gewalten zum Trotz sich erhalten, nimmer sich beugen, kraftig sich zeigen."

Exercise defiance to all terror, never submit to it, show your strength.

Those words planted themselves deep in my mind, and I have lived by them to this day. I'm sure they saved my life over and over again.

At the age of six, Little Heinzchen had his first day at school. Of course that included a visit to the photographer's studio for the traditional picture in knickers and holding a sugarcone. I quickly made friends with three other boys in my class and we began hanging out together whenever we could, which earned us the gangland moniker: "The Four Leaf Clover." Fate would be tough on my friends. Bernd, the youngest, died during an appendectomy when he was ten. Lothar, the oldest, perished in a concentration camp. Ralph made it to Israel, only to pass away in his forties from a lingering illness.

I made other after-school friends in the neighborhood. Our market square was used in the morning for its intended purpose; in the afternoons, after it was washed and cleaned, it was ours to play on. We rode our bicycles around it, played football on it, and otherwise hung out there, always on the lookout for a good fight. The Ruhr was Germany's industrial heartland, and its people were tough. You learned soon enough to ask questions later. At the merest hint of an insult, you attacked. After all, you had to defend your "honor" and territory.

The street fights got bigger and bigger. Armed with bats and sometimes knives, we'd "defend" our neighborhood against all hostile intruders. When we decided that things had got too quiet, we'd resort to a cunning tactic: we'd send the shortest kid in our gang to find our "enemies" and heckle them, while the rest of us hid in doorways, armed and ready. Sooner or later the other gang's patience would run out and they'd punch the little pain-in-the-butt. Right away, the closest "warrior" on our side—usually a tall guy—would step out and declare: "You hit my little brother! You're gonna pay for that!" We'd all come out of our hiding places and the war would be on again.

My parents watched these developments and concluded that Little Heinz had better learn to take care of himself. So during my first year of school they enrolled me in a sports club called Hakoah. That was a highly disciplined organization with a number of departments, including boxing. My specialties were track and field, floor and bar exercises, and swimming. The latter was really my favorite, and by the time I was nine I had earned a certificate for forty-five minutes of endurance swimming.

Of course, the only son in the family had to get a good education, so in 1931 I entered the prestigious Humboldt Gymnasium (high school). To my dismay, my Orthodox mother also forced me to attend after-class religious programs, as well as Sabbath services every week in Essen's beautiful synagogue.

I must add, though, that these rigid requirements were offset by wonderful summer vacations, when I went with my parents to little villages in the Black Forest or stayed and worked with a farm family in the foothills of the Alps.

There were some clouds in the sky, but life was still pretty pleasant for us in Germany.

January 30, 1933: Under strong pressure from the Reichstag, President von Hindenburg appointed a new chancellor. In the afternoon, I had just finished a religious class and was walking with one of my friends, who happened to be the son of Polish Jews who had been driven into Germany by the first pogroms and who had much more experience with persecution than we did. "Extra! Extra!" we heard newsboys screaming on Essen's hectic main square. "Adolf Hitler has become our new chancellor!" I turned to my friend, unconcerned, thinking of our upcoming football game. He looked panic-stricken. "This is bad for us," he insisted. "He's a dangerous anti-Semite." At the time, his words didn't register with me, and I went about my planned day.

Germany's new leader proceeded carefully. He still faced strong political opposition, and he was concerned that other countries might boycott German imports if he revealed his true intentions too soon.

On April 1, 1933, armed stormtroopers posted themselves in front of Jewish-owned stores in our neighborhood holding signs demanding that the German population not patronize these "enemies of the Reich." I remember two guards in front of our main store. They were both from the neighborhood, and we knew they had been unemployed for several years. Also, some Jewish citizens of our city were arrested for invented reasons. But this was early days, and most of them were released shortly afterwards.

The next step was the public burning of books by Jewish authors. Harassment of individual Jews by brown—and black-uniformed punks (S.A. and S.S.) soon became common. It wasn't long before the same thugs began ransacking Jewish homes at gunpoint. They weren't ordered to, they just did. Their excuse was that they were looking for stashed weapons. Most of the time, some desirable items were "confiscated."

The Summer Olympics of 1936 gave us a breather. Berlin was hosting them. When Hindenburg died in 1934, Hitler had declared himself the supreme leader of Germany, the "Fuehrer," and here was the opportunity for his National Socialists to demonstrate to all the world how welcoming, how progressive, how well organized their new Germany was. So the Nazis focused all their efforts on the Games, which temporarily halted the campaign of terror against the Jews and Socialists who were their scapegoats.

My half-sister Irma was managing our second shop when she became engaged to a young man of the Catholic faith. Her choice was hard for my mother to accept. In the end, it was decided that this new member of our family should at least be circumcised. This was not a common practice in Germany at the time, except for religious or health reasons. Anyway, he let it be done, and my parents rewarded the newlyweds by giving them the tobacco shop. Irma and Julius worked hard building the business, until soon they could afford to buy a small D.K.W. automobile. That was the first car in the neighborhood, and I was thrilled. At last, I had a brother (even if he was twelve years older), and even better, he had progressive ideas and a new car.

Meantime, the worsening political situation was starting to touch me directly. The Nazis' *Judenfrei* (Jew-cleansing) policies had reached my school; as a "non-Aryan," I was expelled. Once again, my parents made a wise decision: they contacted a family friend who was an electrical contractor and persuaded him to take me on as an apprentice. I got to really enjoy the work, and as a bonus, enrollment in a trade school was mandatory. Unfortunately, that job lasted only a year, because my boss, who also was Jewish, heeded the political winds and jumped at a fleeting opportunity to immigrate to Uruguay (at that point, Jews were still allowed to immigrate).

Jobs were hard to find in my situation, and we were in no position to be picky. So I switched trades and found a plumbing apprenticeship. It wasn't exactly my choice, but I got used to the work and even got to enjoy it. And again, it meant I could attend a trade school.

By this time, Jews in Germany were being forced to separate themselves from the rest of the population. There was still plenty for us to do in our leisure hours. Around that time, two wildly popular venues were established by the Jews of Essen: the Youth Building, an architectural showcase, and the Café Dreilinden. The former held a huge theater that could be converted in minutes into a gymnasium. It also had a bowling alley, a library, dozens of classrooms and lecture halls, a cafeteria, and a lot of enthusiastic participants. We conducted our youth-group meetings there, played ping-pong, went to gym classes, and attended many cultural events. I even took English classes there during my last few months in Germany. The Dreilinden was a social gathering place. Besides a gourmet restaurant, it had bars and dance floors and was popular with plenty of out-of-towners who didn't have anything like it at home. It was an easy place to make friends.

Another event from those years is still vivid in my memory. On June 22, 1938, Max Schmeling, the former heavyweight world champion, tried to regain his title from Joe Louis, the "Brown Bomber," at Yankee Stadium in New York. The match was heavily promoted in Germany, which expected a political windfall when Schmeling brought the belt home again. To listen to the bout live, we had to stay up till two a.m. My brother-in-law Julius owned a good shortwave receiver, and we all made sure we were in his house at that unearthly hour. But only 124 seconds into the match, the German announcer went into hysterics: "But Max! Max, what are you doing? There must be a mistake, you can't be knocked out yet!" This would be remembered as one of Louis's greatest victories, as well as an early defeat for the Third Reich. As for me, that was when I realized something for the first time: there was another Great Power across the ocean. Maybe in due time there would be plenty more Joe Louises with the strength to free us from the looming tyranny.

I kept working as a plumber's apprentice and was learning quickly. When vacation time came around, Aunt Ida invited me to visit her in Amsterdam. She and her husband had moved there not too long before. This was almost the last chance for me to leave Germany and return as a citizen. It was fascinating to meet people across the border. Most of them had built new albeit modest lives as foreign nationals and were deluding themselves that they were now safe from the Nazis. Unlike in Germany, food was still plentiful in Holland. To earn the money to buy it with was another story.

I returned to Essen. My employer, master plumber Sigmund Schweitzer, was a timid little man who lived modestly with his wife. His two grown sons had already left Germany with their wives. Being an old-timer, he knew his trade thoroughly and taught me a lot. Literacy wasn't his strong suit, so I took over his sons' job of making proposals, writing invoices, and keeping the books.

By now, Jews and political activists were leaving Germany in droves. Our circle of friends kept shrinking. My parents lost their small chain of tobacco shops mainly as a result of boycotts. Only my sister and her "Aryan" husband had been able to hang on to a shop. Around this time they were blessed with a healthy son, Dieter. At last, I had something I never had before—a little brother (a nephew, at least). Meanwhile, my father became a traveling salesman, supplying selected people with his tobacco goods and earning a meager living. By now, even the most optimistic Jews in our city, the ones who had been so sure that this whole thing would blow over, were beginning to take off their blinders.

My parents applied for American visas for our family. They also tried to find a spot for me on a children's transport to Holland, which the Dutch government had just started as a humanitarian gesture.

The nearest American Consulate to us was in Stuttgart, and my father knew only one way to deal with anybody: the straight and honest way.

Unfortunately, my parents never lived to learn the true reason why our registration number wasn't processed by the extremely busy consulate, which by then was being overwhelmed by desperate applicants. Later, when I came to the United States, I noticed that most of ones who were lucky enough to escape Germany in time had lived near American consulates. Some of them admitted to me that they had paid off consular officials to shift their visa applications to the top of the pile.

The Nazis' anti-Jewish laws were becoming more and more unbearable. On October 28, 1938, in the middle of the night, every Polish-born Jew in Germany, including small children, was arrested by the Gestapo. The following morning they were all forced back across the Polish border. Some of my good friends and soccer teammates were among them. They were allowed to take only hand luggage. The rest of their property was confiscated by the Reich.

On November 7, 1938, the German diplomat Ernst vom Rath was assassinated in Paris. The suspect was a seventeen-year-old boy named Herschel Grynzpan. That was a signal for the SA and SS to launch a long-prepared plan. On the night of November 9 and well into the following day, hell broke loose for the Jews in Germany.

Early in the morning of November 10, a sympathetic neighbor hammered on our door to tell us that our beautiful synagogue was on fire and that most Jewish-owned shops and even some houses were being demolished by mobs in brown and black uniforms. On top of that, every known Jew was being threatened with immediate arrest.

My father, cool as always, immediately ordered me to put on my blue overalls, leave the house, and walk out of the neighborhood in my work clothes. I wasn't to go anywhere where people might recognize me. By then there was plenty of excitement on the streets, so it was easy for me to disappear among all the people who had come to watch all the government-endorsed barbarity.

Furniture was flying out of windows, and the most beautiful shops were being trashed, their windows shattered and interiors looted. The most awesome sight, though, was the burning of the great Synagogue of Essen, an architectural masterpiece. Soon after, the Youth Building was destroyed as well.

After this orgy of legalized thuggery, every German man and woman would have to make a choice. (1) Support the gangster government with the excuse that the Fuehrer could do no wrong and was working solely for Germany's good. (2) Hear nothing, see nothing, and say nothing (which is what most Germans chose to do). (3) Join an underground Resistance group (they still existed) and fight these enemies of the human race to the bitter end. Almost no one took this third course, and one can sympathize, because it would have meant almost certain death not just for them but also for their families.

On the afternoon of that tragic day, I called home from a telephone booth. My mother and sister Friedel were alone. They advised me to hold out until dark and then proceed to the apartment of my brother-in-law, where I could spend the night. My father had already gone there, reliable information having reached them that a great number

13

of Jewish men were being arrested for shipment to the prison camp at Dachau (which was not yet a concentration camp).

Under the cover of night, I made my way to my brother-in-law's, in a neighborhood of well-paid skilled workers. There were no individual orders of arrest yet. The day was full of confusion for everyone, and only easy-to-find male Jews were being arrested by the brown and black hordes. I met my father, sister, and brother-in-law, and we decided to shelter there for a few days.

Soon after, the government announced that every man who could obtain a visa to another country would be released from Dachau. What they neglected to add was: "Provided he survives the torture." Those who did, came back with the first horror stories. They had plenty of company in their misery—priests, homosexuals, communists, socialists, gypsies, and, believe it or not, criminals. All of them were known only by their number and by the patch on their zebra uniform, each patch corresponding to their "crime." For example, a red triangle meant a political opponent; green, a criminal; and yellow with the additional imprint of the word "Jude," of course, identified a Jew. There was no guesswork for the SS guards, who could apply their treatment according to each poor devil's category.

A close friend of our family survived this early ordeal in Dachau and talked cautiously about his experiences there a few days before he left Germany. One story he told us still lives in my memory. There was this monk wearing his hat—in itself a provocation for the sadistic guards. They ordered him to plant two poles about a hundred feet apart and hang his hat on one of them. The two poles marked his assigned route, and every time he passed his hat, he had to salute it. They made him walk at first, then run, faster and faster, day and night. When he collapsed, he was reawakened with cold water. He didn't survive to the next day.

When the world learned about the German pogroms, it reacted harshly, and the Nazis stayed their hand for a few weeks. This was my opportunity, my father pointed out to me. Since I was the youngest in the family and still had a lot of living to do, he insisted that I prepare right away to leave for Holland. If I couldn't cross the border legally, I was to find a way to sneak in.

I had two busy weeks ahead of me. I needed to obtain a certificate of a clean police record, proof of good health, and a declaration of personal belongings and finances. After all that, if the Interior Ministry approved my leaving, I would only be able to take 10 marks out of the country.

I also secured certificates from the trade school and my master plumber. When the passport arrived, I received the present of an additional name: Israel, since the government had decided to identify all Jewish men with it, and all women with the name Sarah. It was required to use these names on all documents.

Hitler's racist theories weren't universally popular in Germany. Julius Streicher, the editor of the notorious hate sheet *Der Stürmer,* had a hard time convincing every last German that the Jews were a degenerate race. For his purposes, too many Jews had blonde hair and blue eyes and excelled at sports, just like an Aryans were supposed to. Hence the final insult—to supply these "enemies of the Reich" with uniform names.

On November 30, 1938, I said goodbye to my family and my remaining friends. I was seventeen. I had been spoiled as an only son and youngest child, but I had also been toughened by the last few years of persecution. Now, bets were being taken: "Would he make it?"

I took the permitted carry-on luggage on the train, and also my fortune of 10 marks. A thorough search was conducted at the German bordertown of Emmerich. Though they looked hard, the guards could find no discrepancies: my papers were in order. So I was allowed to leave the "Fatherland."

On the other side of the border, at the Dutch town of Arnhem, I ran into trouble.

2

AMSTERDAM, 1939

T HE DUTCH BORDER patrol was under heavy pressure. Holland was just over the border from Germany's industrial heartland and a preferred escape route for those who were fleeing the Nazis. It also had few natural borders. Even the local people sometimes didn't know which side of the border they were on.

The farmers on either side of the border had developed a good relationship, which meant good communications. They also were quite humane, and besides that, some of them had caught on quickly that a new and highly lucrative business was developing: refugee smuggling. On the German side, border patrols were getting tougher by the day. The Dutch authorities tried to do their duty, but they also, sometimes, looked the other way. Those Germans who made it across the border were registered by the police as political refugees. They had to report to the station, in some cases every day, but no one was ever sent back to Germany unless there was criminal evidence against them.

Holland's armed forces were no match for the Germany's, yet even when the Germans demanded that their political enemies be returned, the Dutch government always refused. The same can't be said for some of Germany's other neighbors, the ones that expected refugees to pay for their refuge.

Holland's economy was struggling in 1938, with unemployment high. Everybody was willing to work for a pittance or to sell their goods cheaply. Yet the Dutch accepted many thousands of political refugees and saved their lives at least temporarily.

A fifteen-minute train ride brought me to the border post at Arnhem. The Dutch guard examined my documents and noticed that my entry papers, written in his language, were not in order. They only entitled me to enter his country as part of a children's transport, not as an individual. In fact, I *had* been accepted as an individual traveler, but my papers hadn't come through by the day I left. If the German border guard had noticed this, he would never have let me leave Germany. Suddenly I was facing a few weeks' bureaucratic delay, and at that moment in history it was likely to cost me my life. Shortly after my departure, the Nazis would begin arresting young Jewish men again.

Luckily for me, I was in Holland now and standing in front of a Dutch border guard. He called one of the many sponsors for political refugees in Arnhem and placed me in his custody for a few days while my official immigration papers arrived from The Hague, the Dutch capital.

My family and I had known about this bureaucratic snag, but we had weighed the odds and decided to gamble because the stakes were so high: my life. We won, and to this day I'm certain that right then and there, at the age of seventeen, I acquired the determination to survive and the confidence to ensure it. That belief in my own survival has never left me.

My sponsor put me on the express train to Amsterdam with heartfelt good wishes. Three hours later I arrived in "Mokem," the nickname that most Amsterdammers applied to their city, a important trade center by the North Sea.

The authorities had by then told Aunt Ida I was coming. Her son, Fred, met me at the station. He was a cheerful, fun-loving guy, ten years my senior, born and raised in Essen just like me. He worked as a traveling salesman, but only when he had to. He had left Germany five years before, right after the Nazi takeover. Because his brother Erich was a cell leader in the Communist Party, his entire family was suspect. After Hitler took power, Erich's life wasn't worth a *pfennig* in Germany. With the help of the KPD, he made it to Holland, only to be interned there after working too hard for the Dutch Communists.

Erich was an intellectual and had read and absorbed *The Communist Manifesto*. And not just read it—he *believed* it and lived by it. His material needs were few. Money and prestige meant nothing to him. He was willing to die for his cause; what mattered to him more than anything else was the opportunity to spread his beliefs.

The Dutch government meant no harm to these idealists. They were content to receive a signed declaration, after a short period of internment, that they considered themselves cured of all radical political beliefs and would never try to undermine the government of their host country. The internment camp was an unnecessary expense to Dutch taxpayers and should have been closed. In any case, all of the detainees eventually agreed to exchange their present lives for more comfortable ones outside the fence.

Except for my Cousin Erich. As a humanitarian solution, the Dutch contacted the Belgian authorities, who agreed to hold him in their last remaining detention center for political radicals. The Belgians, too, intended to close their detention center as soon as they could. Once again, Cousin Erich was the lone holdout. The Belgians waited a little longer and tried hard to convince him that a simple signature would make things so much easier for everyone involved.

The result a few months later: the entire staff turned communist.

Anyway, Fred walked up to me at the station. "Hey, little cousin, it's about time you reached Amsterdam. I've got a couple of girls lined up for you already." So this was the new life waiting for me. Was it truly possible that I could stop feeling persecuted, talk in public to whomever I wanted, about anything I wanted, and even have a date with a girl I liked without being accused of violating race laws?

But first things first. My relatives' apartment was tiny, and they couldn't afford to support an additional member of the family. So the next day I reported to the Refugee Committee, which had been established for the stream of people coming over the border in those days and which was funded by hundreds of private donors. The organization helped both legal and illegal immigrants find affordable housing, apply for work permits (which were difficult to obtain), and contact consulates to expedite visas. The people I saw there granted me the standard amount: seven guilden a week. That was 6.50 for the room I was referred to and 0.50 for pocket money.

Ludwig and his wife Hermintje were my landlords. They owned a dairy store and were very hard-working people. Hermintje was Dutch; her parents ran a poultry shop around the corner. She had given birth to a boy two years earlier. Ludwig was an early refugee from Germany and had spent time in a prison camp before he escaped. Their apartment was above their store in the city centre and had the luxury of three bedrooms. One was assigned to me.

It was a nice small room, and the food was plentiful. My 0.50 a week, though, didn't stretch very far. In a city like Amsterdam there were just too many opportunities for a young man to have a good time. Ludwig was nice about it and let me work for him a few hours a day "off the books." The job involved delivering milk, cheese, and eggs on a heavy bicycle equipped with a large front storage box. To maneuver that rig was a task in itself, but a good challenge for me, and it paid 0.25 an hour. One day I couldn't hold the front wheel in a curve and the milk container turned over, turning the street white.

Other chances arose. People were looking for cheap labor, so I was able to drum up some electrical jobs: replacing fixtures, switches, and outlets, and sometimes doing small installations. Things were starting to look up for me. Soon I was able to buy a used bicycle—my first business investment.

A shoemaker approached me: Would I solicit, collect, and deliver his work on a commission basis? Yes I would, and my income rose accordingly. The streets near the Olympic Stadium, in the southern suburbs, were lined with modern apartment houses that attracted well-to-do immigrants. These were the people who had had the foresight to leave Germany in the earliest days of the Hitler regime, before any restrictions had been placed against "enemies of the Reich." They had been able to liquidate their holdings at fair market prices. They'd even been able to transfer their funds abroad.

These people were used to luxury and could afford it. I rang their doorbells and spoke to the wives who answered in our mother tongue, suggesting that they check the condition of all the shoes in the family. If any repairs were needed, I could offer free pick-up and delivery, as well as a quality job at a fair price. All of which was true, by the way.

My friend the shoemaker was good at his work. He was a Russian emigree who worked, ate, and slept in the same basement room. I got 30 percent of the business I drummed up for him, and both of us prospered.

Once the German and Austrian refugees settled in their new city, they began organizing community activities. One of them was a popular youth center named Ostende. We youth, in turn, formed the Youth Group Ostende. Through them, I got to know many boys and girls my age. Many of us had arrived in Amsterdam only recently and in much the same way I had, so the solidarity was palpable. We organized outings and even overnight trips, held weekly ping-pong tournaments, formed a theater group, and performed for the elders in our community. There was a café on the upper level where people could just hang out and enjoy the delicious Dutch coffee and pastries.

For a time in 1939 I almost forgot that we were all living on top of an active volcano. My parents and my sister Friedel had smuggled themselves over the Dutch border, after failing at several attempts to emigrate legally. As it turned out, my parents wouldn't be allowed to settle in Amsterdam—the new Dutch policy was to spread the refugees out. So they settled in the town of Haarlem, due west on the North Sea coast. That wasn't far, and visiting them always meant an enjoyable hop on the train. Friedel lived close to my place, and we saw each other quite often, since she still felt a moral obligation to look after me, being my elder by ten years. This wasn't always easy for her because, let's face it, I was eighteen years old in a big cosmopolitan city, and my ideas were changing apace. I gave her, too often, a hard time.

There were my two friends, Max and Manfred, and we decided to take off for a week and see and learn a little more about the Netherlands. We prepared our backpacks and sleeping bags and started hitchhiking north. Our goal was to circle the Zuider Zee and return to Amsterdam from the east.

The town of Alkmaar was our first stop. We saw the world-famous cheese market, where merchants transported and offered their cheeses on old-fashioned carriages, dressed in their native costumes. Later in the day we negotiated with a farmer, and he offered to feed us and put us up for the night for a price we couldn't refuse. We liked it so much that we extended our stay by a few days. I don't remember, though, whether our desire to stay was influenced more by the good food, his horses, which he allowed us to ride, or his daughter Mary.

The time had come to continue our journey, so we hitchhiked to Den Helder, then over that masterpiece of engineering, the "Afsluitdijk," the dyke that separates the North Sea from the Zuider Zee, creating vast new lands for agriculture and settlement. It was fascinating to ride along the twenty-mile dyke, which had only two lanes. We felt like we were crossing the ocean on a narrow causeway. Then on to Leeuwarden, Groningen, Zwolle, Amersfoort, and Hilversum on a broad highway back to Amsterdam.

This excursion had introduced us to northern Holland. Now we had a much better idea of what our guest country looked like.

I wasn't broke any more and could start planning my future. I landed a job with an electrical contractor—my first on-the-books job in Holland, complete with work permit. I was making a bit less money, but the job challenged me and was a chance for me to fill in the gaps in my training.

I had made many friends by that point and my social life was hectic. Two favorite spots for my circle were Zandvoort, a beautiful North Sea resort, and the Nieuwemeer, a lake outside the city near Schiphol Airport. Both could be reached by bicycle. Our youth group was well organized and met often. Life almost felt normal. None of us were troubled by the news that the Germans had occupied Czechoslovakia.

September 1, 1939, was a warm late-summer day and led to as pleasant an evening. Friedel threw herself a premature birthday party, and we celebrated in high spirits with the windows thrown open. The radio was blasting, when suddenly the music stopped—

"We interrupt this program with a special message. German troops have invaded Poland. Warsaw has been bombed mercilessly by Stukas. England and France have declared an ultimatum. There will be war if the Germans don't withdraw."

We all stared at one another and decided: "We're west of the German border, Poland is way in the east. Let's keep drinking." The reality was that the German war machine wasn't going to touch our lives for months.

Then, in early 1940, the Wehrmacht invaded Norway and Denmark. Both countries were overrun by German motor divisions within days. For the invaders, it was like taking candy from a child. Those northern countries had been terrified by the events in Poland—that Oslo and Copenhagen would be two more Warsaws.

Finally, the decent people of this world were beginning to realize that pacts and agreements meant nothing to Hitler, who had signed them yesterday only for the sake of breaking them tomorrow. Logic and respect for neighbors no longer existed in Germany. Might now made right, and the Aryans were a "master race." If Hitler wanted a neighbor's raw materials, or saw a military or other advantage for Germany, he invaded without hesitating.

On May 10, 1940, I was asleep. Ludwig, my landlord, always an early riser, pounded hard on my door. "Heinz, get up, the Germans have invaded Holland."

This fact did not surprise me, but the timing was disappointing. I had hoped for another year of freedom, but it wasn't to be. I left for work, just like every other morning. The streets were full of excited people, radios blasting from every window. Everybody had a story to tell. The most popular was that the Germans would never reach Amsterdam: "Holland's defensive system is working." In other words, all the dykes in eastern Holland had been opened and the entire border was being flooded so that the Germans couldn't possibly advance. That was what people were telling themselves.

Later in the day we heard that this invasion had been launched over the entire Western Front: Belgium, Luxembourg, and France. We also were told that Rotterdam had suffered the Warsaw treatment and had been flattened by Stuka bombers, then invaded by paratroopers.

No, little Holland was no match for this military giant, in spite of the heroism of some Dutch army units. Unfortunately, there were also traitors, members of the NSB, the Dutch National Socialist Party. They had infiltrated the army, and some had taken steps to make sure the dikes stayed intact.

It took only days for the Wehrmacht to reach the outskirts of Amsterdam. I was lined up with many other people on the broad Amstelaan Boulevard, near the bridge over the Amstel River, when I first heard the rumble of heavy armor. Then the first tanks crawled across the bridge, followed by trucks towing light artillery. Then came troop transports of different sizes. It was an impressive show: the young German soldiers stared down at us arrogantly, while the Dutch lined the streets in silent awe.

Opportunists were already beginning to collaborate with the invaders. Meanwhile the wheels in my head were spinning. "How much time will my family have to escape again? How long will it take them to catch up with us?"

3
HOLLAND, 1940–42

WE WEREN'T GOING to take chances. I contacted some of my good friends, and we all held an emergency meeting that same afternoon. We decided to run for it that evening.

IJmuiden is the North Sea port for Amsterdam, connected by a dredged channel wide enough to handle even the biggest ocean-going vessels. A road winds along the channel—an hour's journey by bus to the harbor.

We packed only what we had to, knowing we needed to travel light. The Germans couldn't have set any roadblocks yet—the invasion troops had only arrived from the east that day. My friends and I had resolved to move quickly and silently, which meant telling no one—not my parents, not my sister—that we were about to try an escape.

We met as arranged in the northwestern part of the city and boarded the tram. At the last stop on the line we transferred to a bus. Everything seemed normal until we got about halfway and found ourselves in a traffic jam of unknown proportions. It seemed that a lot of people had the same idea as us.

Now, for the first time, I actually *saw* the war. It was ugly, and it would stay that way for the next five years all over Europe. People were fleeing for their lives by bicycle, motorcycle, or on foot, a lucky few by car. Some of them were taking only what they could carry, others were struggling down the highway with as many of their belongings as they could.

We inched our way down to the harbor after dark. One big ship was already jammed with refugees and looked ready to leave at any moment. That's the one we wanted. We had lost too much time already and didn't want to miss the first ship we could board.

After negotiating quickly with the man guarding the gangplank, and agreeing to pay our share and to be satisfied with primitive conditions and overcrowding, he allowed us to board. Supposedly we were heading for England.

Time passed, and the ship didn't move. Then came the news that the ship's owner or his crew were refusing to take the risk of sailing but would be willing to charter or sell the vessel to all its present passengers. That was feasible, since there were a few hundred passengers by now, all of them hoping to save their lives.

But the problem: all the professional sailors had left the ship. Could a crew be drawn from the passengers? Did any of the refugees know how to run a steamship? Calls came through the loudspeaker: "Who knows how to read a nautical chart? Who can handle the helm? Who wants to volunteer for the kitchen?" And so on.

The response wasn't good. It seemed that no one was willing or able to steer hundreds of people safely through U-boat infested waters to England.

Then came the sudden news: "It's too late . . . the Germans have mined the harbor, we're stuck." I will never know if this was the truth on this particular night or only an excuse to save face.

At any rate, our adventure was over. We left the ship disappointed and in low spirits, hoping we could slip back into Amsterdam before dawn, guarding the secret of our failure. Luckily, we found room to squeeze onto a truck heading in that direction. Thanks to my earlier discretion, I was able to tell Ludwig that I'd spent the night partying.

The occupation proceeded slowly. From the German perspective, there was no rush: Holland was already defeated. Meanwhile, there were also military governments to be installed in Belgium and Luxembourg, and the French army, aided by the British, was still showing fight (though not for long).

In Amsterdam, it was business as usual. The Waffen SS troops had moved on to the front lines in France, and the occupying Wehrmacht soldiers who had taken their place were quite tame and more interested in enjoying the good Dutch food and trying to seduce the local girls.

Which wasn't all that easy for them, since at that stage of the war, most of the *meisjes* didn't know yet which direction the winds would be blowing and didn't want to be branded as "Muffenwhore."

The sight of German uniforms and military vehicles became a daily event, and no one paid much attention after a few weeks. For now, the Germans were avoiding provocative actions—all the while, however, robbing little Holland of all its food and raw materials.

Over the next few months, everything looked peaceful in Amsterdam, but I'd been burned before and was getting restless. Around that time, I was offered a maintenance job with the refugee committee. I was hoping to meet influential people regarding emigration overseas, so I took it gladly.

I also moved to new digs, leaving the congested city centre for the newer, southern district of the city. That meant making a new circle of friends, and I fell in with Fred, Leo, and Ludwig. Our friendship began with frequent get-togethers during the days of calm. As the war's dangers intensified, we would grow even closer.

At the age of thirty, after playing the field for years, my sister Friedel decided to marry Julius, who was twelve years her senior. He was a soft-spoken, kind-hearted man. Considering the circumstances, he was also financially comfortable. His work didn't require much education—he was a cattle dealer. That meant he could get his hands on a steady supply of meat, which was starting to become a rare commodity. They invited me over for many good meals that would have been out of reach for me otherwise. They continued to live in my sister's furnished apartment, only a few blocks from my new place.

My parents, though, had to move. The German occupation forces had ordered the local authorities to concentrate their refugees in selected areas. This compelled them to move to Nymwegen, a small town near the German border. The Germans were already arranging things so that they'd be able to sweep up their "enemies" whenever they wanted.

A few weeks later, a public notice was printed in all newspapers and broadcast over all radio stations: "Every resident of the Netherlands must report within two weeks for a population census at the municipal building in his territory." I received a form that looked simple and innocent enough, except for one question at the bottom: "How many Jewish grandparents do you have?"

I hesitated for a minute, but didn't see much danger in the question, so I answered truthfully: "Four." I didn't realize it at the time, but the German occupation authorities would be basing all their actions on those forms. I had missed my first chance to lie to them, but at least—small consolation—so did everyone else I spoke to afterwards. They'd all told the truth as well. None of us had grasped yet that thugs and oppressors don't deserve to be dealt with in honorably. Boy, was I about to learn fast.

A week later, identity cards arrived by registered mail. Once again, an announcement in the papers and on radio: there would be a severe penalty for anyone caught at any time without this card, which carried the holder's photograph.

My identification declared "4 Jewish grandparents" and had a large, stamped letter "J." Suddenly I was marked, and from then on I would have to take pains to avoid situations where my ID might be requested, since showing it would put me automatically at a disadvantage.

I made no progress developing contacts at the Refugee Committee. There was no chance to get on any list for immigration to Chile, Brazil, Uruguay, or Argentina. Those countries had opened their doors briefly, but only early applicants and preselected people were being considered. I had never liked this kind of work and was starting to feel a target on my back, surrounded as I was by so many people who were "enemies of the Reich."

So I switched jobs again. There was plenty of work for an electrical freelancer, especially if he was sharp enough to dig up the needed materials, for which the profits sometimes resulted in higher revenues than the labor charges. I also wanted to learn more about electricity, so I enrolled at a trade school at the same time.

The Battle of Britain was winding down. Now the Royal Air Force was conducting almost nightly bomb runs on military targets in occupied Europe and even into Germany. The shortest path between British air bases and Germany's industrial heartland was directly over Amsterdam. The Luftwaffe had ringed the city with flak guns. Searchlights began scanning the sky as soon as the air-raid sirens sounded. Minutes later, we'd be craning our heads to the rumble and roar of Halifax bombers. It was music to us, and we prayed they wouldn't get hit.

One late evening, the sirens woke me up and I peaked under the blackout shade I'd installed over my window—regulations. I saw a dozen searchlight beams following a target high up in the sky—an RAF bomber flying toward Germany. The ground artillery was growing more intense. It was a beautiful show.

I threw on some clothes and ran down into the street for a better view. An amazing sight—I only hoped the poor devils didn't get hit up there. I was so enthralled that I almost got hit by shrapnel from the flak falling back to earth. Suddenly it was peppering the ground all around me. I picked up a piece and lobbed it in my hand, feeling the heat and weight. Then I dashed back indoors, telling myself never to do *that* again.

The military government was placing more and more restrictions on the population, and a blackout was being enforced every single night, but there was still one theater group left, which kept performing on weekends. A troupe of cabaret performers, all of them refugees from the premier music halls of Berlin and Vienna, was still putting on shows in a small theater on the east side of Amsterdam.

They put on a new program once a month, and my friends and I never missed one of them. For us those shows were an oasis in the desert. It was where I took my dates; it was where I went to see and be seen. I vividly remember a performer from Vienna named Franz Engel, who was the spitting image of Jackie Gleason. You could laugh just by looking at him, and he never failed to ignite the audience with his hilarious performances.

This was the time—the first time—that a girl entered my life. *Truly* entered my life. I'd had plenty of girlfriends before, but they had always been about fun and sex. I met Gisela at the cabaret theater, a dark-haired, brown-eyed beauty of barely 17. She let me chat her up for a minute, but without letting me see through her polished surface. She had class, and I knew right away that I'd better not move too quickly.

I had morning classes in the electrician's school a few times a week and rode my bicycle there, westbound. What a coincidence one morning when I saw Gisela riding the other way, waving hello as she pedaled by. I glanced at my watch to note the exact time and place where we'd crossed paths.

The Samuel's family (left to right) Sali, Step Mother Selma Samuel–Wolf, Sister Inge and Gisela 1942 hiding in Amsterdam

My departure from home the following schooldays was as precise as the Space Shuttle launches at Cape Canaveral. After a few days I had the pleasure of seeing her again. Little by little, by coincidence or design, we started passing each other every schoolday. By then she was appearing in my dreams.

Then came the big day. She stopped, telling me she was a little early and could chat for a few minutes. I learned that she lived with her parents the Samuel's and her sister Inge near my school and that she went to work every morning in my neighborhood.

I invited her on a bicycling date that weekend, and picked her up at her house. We road our bikes to the outskirts of the city and took a long rest on the grass, staring at each other and learning a little more about each other. Little by little over the coming weeks, we fell in love. The moments we spent on the edge of the city watching the planes leaving Schipol Airport became precious for both of us.

1941 was slipping toward 1942. The German armies had stalled in their invasion of Russia and were being destroyed by the harsh eastern winter. The Dutch had been treated gently so far by the standards of the "Master Race." With disaster brewing in the east, it seemed as if the time had come for the conquerors to show the Dutch who was boss.

One late afternoon I was on my way home from a job I'd just finished, just cruising along on my bike. About two blocks from home, one of my friends, Kurt, who lived nearby, came running up to me, shouting: "Heinz, stop! Two guys in civvies are pacing in front of your building. It has to be you they want." I stopped to hear him out and learned that scores of young men, some "politicals" but mostly Jews, were being swept up that afternoon to fill the new concentration camp at Mauthausen in the Austrian Alps. I made a long detour to spy on my house from a distance—sure enough, two men were waiting in front of my apartment, and from their appearance and attitude they were obviously Gestapo.

I pedaled back. "Thanks, Kurt, you've been a friend today." I rode on to my cousins, Hannes and Berta, not too far from my apartment. They welcomed me, agreeing that it was a good idea to let them shelter me. They were a mixed marriage, Jewish and Christian, and a little older, so they weren't in danger of being arrested that day.

Cousin Hannes, a professional accountant, was an intellectual who spoke and wrote in five languages. He kept himself well informed about the political situation in Europe. He knew that Reinhard Heydrich, the Gestapo chief nicknamed "The Hangman," had just been assassinated in Lidice, Czechoslovakia. Besides murdering three hundred Czechs and destroying the town in reprisal, the Gestapo was using that event as an excuse to stomp hard on other Axis-occupied countries, hence that day's arrests.

The war also had some positive effects. So far the relationship between me and these cousins had been very casual. During those testing years, I would observe that the good and the bad in people became amplified under stress—good people became better, bad ones became worse.

Without hesitating, and knowing full well that the Gestapo was looking for me, Hannes and Berta invited me in for dinner and insisted that I stay with them until the heat died down. Luckily for me, the Gestapo was only making a general sweep that day—so far, at least, I wasn't on anyone's arrest list. Hannes' contacts had been able to learn that much for me. So I was able to return to my apartment after a week.

37

The German occupation forces were digging in deep now. One event followed another. In early 1942, a new directive was announced on the radio and in the papers: "Effective in one week, all residents who show four Jewish grandparents on their identity card have to pick up several yellow Stars of David with the inscription "JOOD" (Jew) at the German Occupation Headquarters, and sew them on any outer garments to be worn, on the left side, above the heart. Noncompliance will be punished severely."

I was about to be branded, and I didn't like it at all. The Dutch people reacted immediately, and many of them wore the yellow star voluntarily in order to confuse the authorities. On the first day this new law came into force, a general strike broke out, affecting every phase of life in Amsterdam. The streetcars and trains stopped running, mail delivery halted, and police and firemen called in sick. It was an impressive demonstration of solidarity, and the German occupiers were furious. They staged a show of power, flooding the city with troops and using force when necessary to restore their notion of law and order. The courageous participants of this general strike held out for 24 hours, until their lives were threatened, but they had won just by making their point.

I didn't have the slightest intention of showing a star in public. I camouflaged it, sometimes by wearing an open overcoat casually flopping in the wind, sometimes by carrying an attaché case in front of it. For the casual observer, there was no star; for the investigating authorities, who were popping up more and more often on all street corners, I was wearing the star.

A few weeks later a curfew was declared for all Jews in Holland. None of us were allowed on the streets after 8 p.m. Not only that, but all movie houses, theaters, restaurants, and other public spaces were now off limits, and those places had to display the sign FOR JOODEN VERBODEN (Prohibited for Jews).

An optimist can find a silver lining anywhere. We knew things were getting very tough for us, but since the evenings had become long for us, we might as well enjoy them. All-night poker parties sprang up now that there was no place to go. Quite often I found myself stranded at someone else's house after curfew, with pleasant company. My love life certainly improved.

Fred, Leo, and Ludwig became important to me. We lived in the same neighborhood and were throwing all-night parties for any excuse. Ludwig came in especially handy, because he had a big apartment, once occupied by his older brother, who unfortunately had been caught in the Mauthausen Sweep that I'd barely escaped.

By then, the Jews living in Germany were being deported by the thousands, and we would soon learn that all actions taken against them would be taken in the occupied countries a little later.

Cousin Hannes developed an unusual plan that would save the lives of a few hundred people. When one of his Jewish clients was about to be swept up, he would find a man of Aryan blood who was willing to swear that he had fathered that client out of wedlock—in other words, the client had only two Jewish grandparents. Also, it was sometimes possible to arrange a certificate from the Dutch municipal office—already infiltrated by then with members of the Dutch Resistance—stating that your father had been of "Aryan" blood. At the time, schemes like these only delayed deportation, but as it turned out, these people—unless they got hooked for other political "offences"—were never touched because of their Jewish heritage.

I felt uncomfortable dealing with the authorities in those days, so I chose another route. I made contact with a dealer in identity cards, supplied him with my photo, paid him hundred guilder down (which tapped me out for the time being), and agreed to pay the balance of another hundred at the time of delivery.

The idea was to steal someone else's clean "Aryan" card, replace his picture, and fill in the legal stamp, which was partly on the page and partly on the photo. It took a superb artist to do it well, since the cards used specially impregnated paper stock. My name, of course, would have to match the document, so I became Mr. Jon Blau.

Around the same time, a patriotic Dutch family promised me a place to hide while I began a new life. I could come to them as soon as I received a deportation notice.

In July 1942, well, it happened. I got a letter in the mail: "Mr. Heinz Goldschmitt, you are hereby notified to appear on July 15th, 1942, at 8 a.m. in our office and make yourself available for a special work detail, which could be in another country. Luggage restrictions are twenty pounds; please restrict yourself to necessities only. In case you have heard any rumors, that this summons has any other purpose, please disregard. I can assure you that our only objective is your productive participation in our war effort, and you will be treated in a decent and humane manner." Signed: Aus Der Fuenten, Commander for the Regional Work Brigades.

"Bullshit," I told myself, and some of my better-informed friends agreed with me after reading that letter. We found out later that the same summons had gone to 1,500 people in Holland to fill up the first mass transport, which passed through a Dutch transit camp near Westerbork before continuing to Auschwitz.

Fortunately, the letter provided one week's notice. During that time I received threats from other people who had been called up for the same transport. They knew me well enough to be certain I wouldn't show up. That would make things worse for all of them, so if I failed to appear, they'd blow the whistle on me.

But *other* people were talking about going underground and asking me for contacts and advice. I really didn't have much to offer along those lines, since I wasn't sure myself whether the forgers I'd contacted would hold up their end of the deal. But I told some people what I knew, and let them decide whether the risk was worth taking, if they could afford it at all.

Sadly, on July 15, 1942, only ten people did not show up for the transport. The other 1,490 poor devils placed their heads willingly on the butcher's block. So we learned later.

The day before, I had received my new identity card by paying the balance of a hundred guilders. This time, Commander Aus Der Fuenten would have to leave without me.

4

THE BIG TEST

I T WAS A hot summer day; a couple of hours after I'd failed to show up for the transport. Carrying only a small suitcase, I was running in circles through war-torn Amsterdam. Many young Dutch men had already been drafted for forced labor in German factories. Store shelves were emptying, with the country being plundered by the invaders. An evening blackout of windows and vehicles was being strictly enforced.

The Germans had set up checkpoints to make sure everyone was living up to their regulations. In that they had some enthusiastic help, mainly from the ranks of the NSB, the Dutch Nazi Party.

Cautiously, I approached the contacts that had been given to me for temporary shelter in different parts of the city. One of them told me when I appeared that the promise was a few months old and that meantime, a relative had moved in. Another insisted that he had never made such a promise. The excuses varied as I tried one home after the next. I well knew that my request for a hiding place from the Gestapo was an enormous one. I understood why so few people were willing to expose themselves and their families to internment in a concentration camp and possibly even death.

Late in the afternoon I realized that I had to change tack. I couldn't depend on anyone's help, and I needed to start a new life in a new place, so I decided to pretend that I really was Jon Blau, like my ID card said.

I pulled out the card and studied it to rehearse my date and place of birth, as well as the names of my parents. To my dismay, I found that the artist had done a lousy job on the stamp. It was good enough to pass a routine inspection, but if someone suspected me to start with, I wouldn't stand a chance. So I knew that my conduct would have to be letter perfect, since it was the only ID card I had for now. I set some rules for myself: act as normal as possible, don't look guilty, keep eyes open, and try to avoid checkpoints.

I had memorized the addresses of a few farmers in southern Holland, people who had once sold cattle to my new brother-in-law, Julius. The Dutch train system was efficient and still intact—for their own purposes, the Germans wanted to keep it that way. Trains were running late into the night. So I made my way to Amsterdam's Central Station.

Everything looked eerily normal. I saw German soldiers waiting for their connections to the south, and civilians on business trips. I bought a ticket for Eindhoven, boarded it cautiously, found a window seat, and was soon on my way.

It was a pleasant summer evening. Through the window, I watched the peaceful scenery of the lowlands pass by. For the first time in days, after all the tense preparations, I felt relaxed and composed. Mostly, I was consumed with the desire to survive this war. I must have dozed off, because when I opened my eyes again the train was slowing down and entering a station. In the dim light, I could just read the sign: EINDHOVEN.

It was quite common at that time for travelers to spend the night in the waiting rooms of railroad stations, since hotels were too expensive for most people. So along with most of the passengers, that's what I did. It was too late for any other connection anyway.

First, though, I placed a telephone call to my sister in Amsterdam, who was deeply worried about my adventure and afraid to become a victim herself on one of the next transports, which she knew from reliable sources were already being organized. I encouraged her not to give up and to find a hiding place with her husband, especially since they could afford to pay for one. She promised to start looking right away.

Our conversation on a public telephone wouldn't have been very clear to an outsider. All of us had developed Aesopic language—words that on the surface had an entirely different meaning than intended. For example: a storm coming in meant arrests had started again. None, half, or full Jewish were indicated with the numbers 20,

19, and 18 respectively. As soon as my parents learned my new name and post office box, they began addressing me as "Dear Friend." Monetary matters were coded by replacing the numbers with the letters of our family name in sequence: 1=G, 2=O, 5=S, and so on.

I found a spot on a bench in the half-full waiting room and stretched out my legs. The night passed uneventfully. At one point the German military police, known as the "Kettenhunde" because of the heavy badges they wore on chains around the neck, came in and checked all the uniformed Germans for proper travel documents.

At the crack of dawn I boarded a bus in front of the station, which took me to a rural area 45 minutes away. I knew that some farms in the district were large enough that they would be hiring field hands for the coming harvest.

By that point, many Dutch men had been drafted for war production in Germany. I hoped I'd be able to awaken a farmer's patriotism by telling him that I, too, had been drafted but, being a good Dutchman, preferred to work Dutch soil.

My second attempt succeeded. This was only a family farm: father, mother, a grown-up son and daughter, and a grandmother, who used to relieve herself in the barn. They jumped at the chance to hire a young man for the harvest. They would pay me half a guilder a week with free room and board, which would mean sharing a bed with the son.

The meals were unusual, at least for me. There was always a single dish, which was placed in the middle of the table. Everyone sat around it with a fork, and dove in. At first I often left the table a little hungry, but it didn't take long to develop good timing and the proper level of aggression.

The family's favorite topic was the escape of the Dutch Royal Family to England, which enabled them to fill their stomachs with the best food, while we who were left behind in Holland had to make do with less than we were used to.

For my part, I counted my blessings and appreciated each day of freedom, fresh country air, and enough to eat. The farm work was a little boring, though it had some interesting moments. One day I witnessed the birth of a calf—a very difficult one, according to the attending veterinarian. It took about three hours, and it was fascinating to watch the newcomer to this world slowly leave its mother's womb. Everyone helped extract the animal and was soaking with sweat by the end.

After a few weeks on the farm, my boss pressured me into reporting my new residence to the police in the nearby village. Fortunately, he was too busy to accompany me and would have to take me at my word. I borrowed a bicycle and pedaled into town. It was bad enough that some people in the village stared at me simply because I was a stranger. I went nowhere near the police station, of course. Instead I tried to establish contact with a few trusted people. I went to the post office and set up a box, then wrote a few lines to my parents, my sister, my friend Ludwig, and Gisela.

I also checked out the only movie house in town, since I wasn't expected to work on Sundays. All media, of course, were censored, but I had learned by now to read newspapers between the lines. Now I hoped to learn to do the same with newsreels to get an accurate sense of the war's progress.

When I returned to the farm, my employer asked, "Did you register, Jon?" and breathed relief when I lied that I had. For the next few weeks I worked from dawn to dusk, stopping only for meals and sleep. Sunday afternoons or evenings I went to the movies.

Soon enough, I began receiving letters, first from my parents, who told me they were still all right in Nymwegen, though worried they might soon be deported. Then a letter from Ludwig, another of the handful who had ignored the summons for the transport. He was holding his own in Amsterdam. Using the name on his false ID card, he had rented a small furnished room in the western suburbs, in a blue-collar neighborhood. He felt quite safe there, but he complained about the food and his financial situation. He tried to convince me to return to the city, where we could mingle with the crowds and perhaps find a way to make a few bucks and even have a little fun. He also had some bad news for me: my sister and her husband had been deported. He had contacted their landlord, and this is what they had told him—

Late one evening the Gestapo came to their apartment asking for them. As had been rehearsed before, the landlord told them in a loud voice: "I think they're sleeping somewhere else tonight." Friedel and Julius, who lived upstairs, heard him and hid quickly in a large closet in the attic, which was blocked by storage items—trunks, old furniture, linen, and so on. The hiding place was good enough to convince the "Supermen" that their victims weren't there. They were about to leave when they heard a nervous cough from the closet. My brother-in-law just couldn't take the pressure for another minute, and both of them were found and arrested.

The good news came from Gisela, who had found a way for us to meet the following Sunday. She told me when she would be arriving at the local railroad station. I was able to get there by bus, and we went for a long hike. It was an exciting moment for both of us—I felt things I never had before. Perhaps deep inside, we both sensed that this was the last time we would see each other during this war.

Back at work the following day, I felt restless and realized that this hiding place couldn't last forever. I was also tired of this small farming community, its small-town habits and attitudes. I stayed until the harvest was in and then asked for a leave of absence. The farmer was happy to grant it: the work by this point could be handled by the family, and I would only be a parasite if I stayed.

My spirits were high. I was completely confident in my new identity—sometimes I myself believed I was Jon Blau. On the return train to Amsterdam, I tried to avoid any dealings with the authorities, since my ID was a little shaky. My first task in the city would be to get better documents, whatever it took.

I arrived at the central station in the early evening and took the tram to Jan Evertsen Straat in the western suburbs, where Ludwig had a furnished room. He had a new name, too—Willem Poppel. Fortunately I found him at home.

We had plenty to talk about, and we sat up half the night to develop a new survival strategy.

The next morning I picked up a newspaper and combed through the classified ads. Furnished rooms were being offered at reasonable prices in the immediate neighborhood.

Mevrouw Van Ruyven, a divorcee, was living with her teenaged daughter Elly on the second floor of a typical (for Amsterdam) apartment house. An attic room with a separate entrance two flights higher was part of her lease holding. She had no use for it, and in her present situation she would welcome the extra income.

It was perfect for me. She would never see when I left or returned home, or who I was with, or what I was carrying. She was also the most liberal woman one could imagine. Once she had gained a little trust in me, she would invite me to listen with her to Radio Moscow's shortwave broadcasts—a "crime" that promised severe punishment. That is, if you were caught.

So we listened together a few times a week. Now I could always glean the true state of the war, by comparing the Russian bulletins with the German ones. Later on, I learned why she never listened to the BBC instead. She belonged to the Communist Party and was a political idealist. I often saw people making brief visits to her apartment. They all had the nervous, haunted look of fugitives. By now I had become an expert in that category.

Many evenings the three of us would sit together over coffee and cookies, listening to the forbidden shortwave stations. Elly was a mature 15-year-old who played classical music on the piano during intermissions. One night Mevrouw told me: "Jon, if you turn me in, I'll have you killed." I loved both of them, and I was never sure whether they knew my true identity and just avoided the subject or believed my story—that I was a Dutch patriot who never would work for the Germans.

So I'd found a perfect place to live. But I still had two problems to solve: Where was I going to find work? And how was I going to arrange a better ID? The first problem solved itself quickly enough. I heard that an old acquaintance, Martin, had begun manufacturing toys. Always the entrepreneur, he had come up with a process that required minimal raw materials, mainly paint and scrap wood. Now orders were pouring in, even from Germany. His problem was finding enough workers. He always had been brave, fearing nothing and on one. So at that point he was desperate for workers and looking for good deeds to perform. Knowing my true identity, he hired not only me but Ludwig as well. He simply told us: "I hear no evil and see no evil, I have checked your ID cards and entered you on the company payroll. After the proper deductions, you're on your own."

The final problem, a new ID, was more difficult to crack. My contacts told me they had made tremendous progress in obtaining good ink and rubber stamps and that they could convert any identity card to perfection for a new owner. Unfortunately, the documents themselves had to come from people who actually existed, and they couldn't steal them quickly enough to meet the growing demand. Which meant, of course, that the prices had soared.

Since I couldn't afford to buy a stolen card, I would have to steal one myself. I began visiting a public swimming pool in the neighborhood. There were plenty of changing cubicles around the pool, and the ones with locks cost a little more. Because their walls didn't reach the ceiling, it was possible, if you were athletic and desperate enough, to climb from one to the next. On weekdays it was easier to find an empty one next to whichever one I selected.

Patience was my motto: I waited for a victim as close as possible to my age, height, and weight, since the fewest changes would make for the most authentic document. The most time I ever spent in the water was while I was looking for Mr. Right.

Then came the big moment: I saw young fellow who was definitely a good candidate, so I selected a cubicle right next to his. A moment later, he came out in his bathing trunks and slammed the door behind him. Fortunately, he was also very active in the pool, swimming laps. I jumped out right away and disappeared into the empty cell, locking the door behind me. Climbing over the top was a piece of cake. My frantic search through his pockets was rewarded with a trophy: his ID card.

"Sorry, old boy," my conscience told him, "for putting you through the trouble of reporting a lost document. I hope you don't mind, because it could save my life, thank you."

So my new last name became Martin. Since my artist had become expert at altering documents, we changed the first name to my real one: Heinz. I had this done for several reasons: 1. It was the name I went by among the few people I still ran into, who knew me from before the war. 2. It was a typical German name, which would buttress my story that my mother was German, in case someone questioned my accent. 3. It would dampen suspicions in the village where I had worked for a few months.

My employer fired Jon Blau and hired Heinz Martin. By then, things were going well at the factory. I had become a foreman in my department, sanding wooden animals, and we were working at high capacity to fill all the Christmas orders. There was plenty of overtime, so we were making a good living. Once in a while we could even afford to go out on the town. On Saturday nights we'd stroll up and down Kalver Straat, looking for girls to pick up. Back then, every city in Europe had a Kalver Straat—a pedestrian zone lined with stores, restaurants, and entertainment spots, where boys and girls could look for each other. For a change, life was normal again, and we could almost forget that we were hunted men.

It was New Year's Eve, 1942. Ludwig, myself, and Jonny, a friend who was also hiding from the Germans, and whom I had placed in our factory, were out walking near the busy Munt Plein. We had just had dinner together and were in high spirits. I must have been speaking German, because all of a sudden, through the crowds, two tall men in German uniforms, wearing plaques with heavy chains on their chests, pushed through and stopped us.

"Ausweise bitte!" Your IDs, please.

After an instant's shock, I recovered and thought: "Where the hell did they come from? What's on their minds? They're *Kettenhunde*, so they must suspect us of being German deserters. If our documents hold up, we have it made."

The next ten minutes felt like ten years. They inspected those papers from top to bottom, focusing their flashlights on specific areas, discussing us with each other—"What do you think?"—and not reaching any conclusions. They couldn't find any evidence of counterfeit, but they smelled something fishy. They began questioning me specifically: "How come you're a Hollander and speak perfect German?" Recognizing the importance of the answer, and reading their minds, I replied with a sneer, completely unlike a real German: "Don't you see my first name? My mother was German, and she taught me to speak it when I was a kid."

Somehow, they bought it. They might not be fully convinced, but the show must go on, and on a night this busy there must be easier cases than ours to tackle. So they let us pass on.

"Happy New Year, not to you bastards, but to Churchill, Roosevelt, Stalin, De Gaulle, and all the Allies." That was our resolution, on this night that we had survived the big test.

5

TO BE OR NOT TO BE

THE NEW YEAR began badly. The first week, I received a card: "Dear Friend, the weather here in Nymwegen has been very bad. Tonight we were surprised by a severe thunderstorm and had to evacuate the house. We left our belongings with the Beckers. Hope to see you when all is over. Your true friends."

My parents had been arrested at the age of 60 and were on their way to the transit camp at Westerbork. They had to leave most of their belongings with their landlords, since they were only permitted to take what they could carry with them. By that time, reports were leaking out about the conditions in Dutch and other European concentration camps—camps with strange and disturbing names, like Auschwitz, Birkenau, Lublin, and Theresienstadt.

I was told that the Reich's Dutch prisoners were staying only days in Westerbork before being sorted into categories and sent east to the big Polish camps. For the elderly, like my parents, there would have been only one chance for survival: Theresienstadt. That camp was for "privileged" Jews and by Nazi standards was almost a sanatorium. It was almost impossible to arrange entry there. After the war, I encountered only one category of survivors from this camp: "Disabled German Veterans from World War I." The rest of the Theresienstadt survivors had some means of persuasion: good German contacts, or fat bank accounts in Switzerland. Or in some cases they were willing to grant sexual favours.

The toy factory was still busy, but only a few young people were lucky enough to be allowed to work in Holland. Everyone else was being conscripted for defense work in Germany. After the Russians crushed the Germans at Stalingrad in February 1943, the occupation forces in Holland became very nervous and increased the rewards for those who would inform on fugitives from the Gestapo.

Once a week I had dinner with a couple from Hamburg. The husband had been saved by my cousin Hannes' documentation ploy. It was always a pleasant get-together. They mentioned quite often how lucky I was to be at liberty and working while they had a hard time making ends meet.

By then I was renting a second room in downtown Amsterdam, which I used only for entertainment—I hardly ever spent a full night there. It was a place to register with my identity card so that my true residence would remain hidden.

This was the height of arrests, deportations, and slave labor recruitment. There was almost no one left in the country who hadn't been forced into one of three categories: (A) The guardians, who had volunteered to work for the Germans, including the Nazi Party. (B) The guarded—that is, most of the Dutch—who were terrified of being informed on for the slightest reason, when they weren't themselves informers. Most of them, by the way, were going to bed hungry by that year. (C) The Dutch Resistance, a fascinating bunch whose numbers were growing. They came from all walks of life and had joined up for all different reasons.

Some of the people in the Resistance were in it for themselves, to save their own skins, and let others do the dangerous work. Others were full of fire to battle the common enemy and were ready at any time to place themselves in danger. And some were both, at one time or another.

I had many meals with Hannes and Berta. Their door was always open to me, and a brother or sister couldn't have shown more love. They trusted me to be careful not to be followed to their place, and so far there hadn't been one incident.

July 1943, a hot summer afternoon. I could have celebrated my first anniversary of successfully escaping deportation. Instead, I was working in the toy factory on the third floor, minding my own business. Through a window, I saw a big black limousine pull up. Two civilians got out of it—perhaps some German big-shot customers? A moment later, the telephone rang in our department. Martin wanted to talk to me: "Heinz, there's someone to see you. Come down immediately." Thoughts raced through my mind. Could somebody really be looking for me? Would Martin call me down like this without giving me warning? Should I try to get away through a window?

No, it was impossible—Martin sounded very cool and confident. This had to be a routine meeting, and I couldn't let him down. I went down to his office, where he and two sinister-looking characters awaited me.

One of them got up and approached me. "Are you Heinz Martin?"

"Yes," I replied in the coolest possible voice.

"Let me see your Personsbewijs!"

"In what capacity?" I asked.

"Gestapo." He flashed a badge.

"Boy, this is serious," I thought. "I'll have to play the game all the way now."

I presented my ID card. He looked at it grudgingly, examining it, his partner looking over his shoulder. "Looks all right," he said, "but you still have to come with us to headquarters. We have a personal complaint against you."

I looked at Martin, who shrugged his shoulders. Then I pulled myself together and called the bluff.

"Okay," I said, "let's go. I'm not guilty of anything." I watched their faces, and they looked confused for a minute. Even so, they led me to their big black limo, this time without handcuffs, and drove to the infamous Gestapo headquarters on Mervede Straat near the Olympic Stadium.

While my two guards were leading me up the wide concrete stairs, I saw descending a high-ranking officer flanked by a handful of underlings. I blinked—it was Commander Aus Der Fuenten in the flesh. His photo was in all the newspapers by now. He was second in authority to Seiss Inquart himself, the high commander of Occupied Holland, and was widely and deeply feared.

Anxious not to miss the chance, I tore myself loose and approached him. "Herr Obersturmbannführer," I told him with an even voice. "There's been a terrible mistake. Your men are questioning me in a mix-up of identity, and I'm missing valuable time in a factory, producing toys for German children."

He stared at me for a moment, then at his underlings, asking them: "Who is handling this case?"

"Gruppenführer Henkel, Herr Obersturmbannführer," they answered, clicking their heels.

Turning to me again, he assured me: "Don't worry. He's a good man who will resolve this case efficiently."

That's what I was afraid of. The *Gruppenfuehrer* was awaiting me at his desk with a letter in front of him. The handwriting looked familiar—large, drawn-out letters, very unique, easily identified. I had seen it before. The sender had to be my host, the lady from Hamburg who fed me once a week, and who was well aware of my true identity and hungry for the reward.

He opened his interrogation with a facetious smile. "Let me see your ID, Heinz Martin." After glancing at it, he roared at me: "You fucking liar! Your real name is Heinz Goldschmitt and you're wanted by us."

I was ready for that and kept my cool. "Herr Gruppenführer, do you believe the contents of this letter in front of you, written by a money-hungry, desperate woman who invented this story?"

He looked at me with surprise and said: "We'll get to the truth." He turned to his hangmen. "Take him to the Schouburg and investigate." The Shouburg was a theater that had been converted into a prison.

Back I went into the black limo, this time handcuffed and with one guard honoring me with his company in the back seat. They took me to another district of Amsterdam, this one across from the zoo, where the Shouburg was located. The streets looked inviting; people were still out enjoying the beautiful summer weather.

Would this be my last glance of freedom, possibly even the end of my life? "No," I told myself, "it can't be, it must *not* be. I'm young and strong, I'll challenge these brown and black hordes, I'll fight them till my last breath with any weapon I can find."

At the Schouburg, my guards handed me over to the SS commander with these words: "Another one for you. This one's tricky and still under investigation. You know what to do."

He nodded and pushed me inside, taking my handcuffs off. Then he told me: "Get used to your quarters, then you and I will have a little talk."

I looked around and was pleasantly surprised. The theater was heavily guarded by SS troops but was far from secure, the way a purpose-built prison would have been. My instincts told me straight away: "There must be a bolt hole somewhere." I also saw that some of the guard duties had been trusted to the Joodse Raad, a handful of Jews who had been held back for the last transport in return for helping the SS with the final deportations.

It didn't take long before I spotted an old friend. Paul was wearing a yellow band on his arm, which marked him as an official, not a prisoner. He was realistic enough to know that this privilege only bought him time—it wasn't going to save his life. As it turned out, everyone in this group would be deported within weeks.

Paul gave me a friendly welcome and pulled me into a corner, with a pad and pencil out so that he could pretend he was interrogating me for the next transport.

"Heinz," he said, "I know you've been on the run for a whole year, that you have contacts in the underground, and I need you. This shitty job won't last much longer, and then it's going to be my turn. I have to escape before the last transport. Right now I'm still allowed off the premises for official reasons. One hand washes other, so let me know what you need from the outside."

I knew well that in these desperate times, informers weren't exactly rare anymore, so I was cautious at first. I asked him just one question: "Paul, when is the next transport due?"

"In about ten days, to Westerbork," he answered.

"Thanks, Paul. That gives us plenty of time. I'll get back to you."

In the theater, all of the seats had been taken out. The main floor and the mezzanine were packed with prisoners, including entire families. The food was adequate, and blankets were available to sleep on the floor. We were allowed to use the bathrooms in the morning to wash up and could even take a half-hour walk every afternoon in the small yard.

The surrounding streets were densely populated, and I already knew them well. I had only one thought: Escape! As quickly and efficiently as I could. During the first night, I didn't close my eyes. I picked a spot right beside the stage and slowly and carefully, using my blanket as cover, began probing the floor boards. I couldn't afford to arouse any suspicion. It was still early in the game, and several options were likely open to me. In any case, I found no weak spots in the floor that night.

Next morning, just after roll call, which was conducted twice a day, I heard my name blasted over the speaker. The

Kommandant wanted to see me. He was waiting for me in his office, which had once been a dressing room. "We searched your room at the address that is entered on your identity card. It's almost empty and your landlord only saw you once while you were renting the place. So you're lying again, and if you know what's good for you, you'll tell me your real address immediately!"

I hesitated, recalling the methods the SS used to squeeze the truth out of their prisoners. Then I pictured that beautiful, safe room with Mevrouw and Elly, and I told myself, "Never will I give them up."

I looked my hangman straight in the eye and answered: "Herr Kommandant, unfortunately those are all my possessions, and that is my real residence."

His punch sent me across the room. Then he laid into me with his boots.

When he was finished, he released me with these words: "You swine! I've got plenty of time to get the truth out of you. See you tomorrow."

It was one of the Germans' favorite tactics to show a prisoner to the other inmates right after a bloody interrogation. It set an example of what would happen to anybody who violated their rules. I got a few sympathetic remarks and questions from my fellow prisoners, but I brushed them off to focus all my thoughts on escaping. For a brief time I tried to organize a group of the youngest, strongest prisoners to simply storm out of the building at an opportune time, when only one or two guards would have to be overpowered. Once we were all outside, we'd have good chances to vanish in the local crowds. The other prisoners seemed enthusiastic at first, before coming up to me one by one with reservations and excuses.

A few days passed, and to my relief I wasn't called back to the *Kommandant*. He probably had his hands full organizing the coming transport. Tables were set up on the stage, and one by one all of us were interrogated at length about our property. Instructions about luggage restrictions were handed out to us, along with orders where to send the rest of our belongings.

Paul reassured me that I would see a chance to escape at the train station, if I kept my wits about me. I found little comfort in that idea.

Three days before the transport, something happened that helped me reach a decision. A surprise roll call was held in the mid-afternoon. Moments later an inmate was brought in, screaming and groaning, black and blue, bleeding all over and still being beaten by the guards. The *Kommandant* entered right after and declared: "Let this be a lesson to anyone who has the slightest notion of escape. This is only the beginning—the next one caught will be sorry to be alive!"

This was interesting. The man had actually got out of the building and had been caught outside. I had to find out how he'd done it. When he was mingling with the other prisoners again, I approached him cautiously. He was in severe pain but willing to talk to me.

"Would you believe it?" he said. "I got out through the bathroom window behind the stage, jumped into the yard, then over the fence, and through a neighbor's house. That's where I got stopped. Three people overpowered me, picked up the phone, and held me until the guards arrived."

"Were they armed?"

"No."

"Better luck next time," I told him. "Don't give up."

This was good news: there was a window in the building that wasn't barred. But how to get into the bathroom? I knew that the houses on this block were all attached and had small backyards. Once outside, there was no other way to the street except by walking through someone's rear door and out the front onto the boulevard, which was served by tram.

Time was running out for me. I'd have to try the same window, and any civilian trying to stop me, unless he had a gun, had better watch out.

I found Paul the next day.

"Tell me about the bathroom behind the stage," I told him.

"It's being used for storage," he explained. "The door's always locked because the window doesn't have any bars."

"Can you do two things for me? If you do, I'll make sure you'll be riding high with our Resistance group. First, bring in the biggest pocketknife you can find. Second, arrange for the bathroom door to be open tomorrow, for most of the day, which is going to be hectic anyway with all the preparations for the transport."

"It will take some ingenuity, but I think I can handle it."

T-day minus 1. A long table had been placed in the center of the stage. Sitting at it were several members of the Joodse Raad, facing the theater, flanked by two guards. They were calling out names from long lists and interrogating three or four prisoners at a time. The goal, for the Germans, was to get their hands on as much booty as possible—anything the transportees would have to leave behind.

I was watching all of this closely and had noticed that everyone at the table was focusing hard on the task at hand. The door to freedom must be right behind them. My mind was spinning. Paul found me later in the morning, slipped me a good-sized pocketknife, and whispered: "The door's unlocked. Chances are good we can keep it that way, with all the commotion."

The exercise yard was just to the right of the stage. The fences had long since been replaced by high walls. During the half hour we used to walk out there each day, there was always an armed guard blocking entry to it.

Early afternoon. Luckily for me, the exercise break had been called as usual. I was part of the first group, which walked across the stage and into the yard. We started walking. The guard, as always, was in his position at the exit. Behind him on the stage, the large table with all its busy occupants was in full view. A new name was called, whose bearer was outside with us. He proceeded to the exit and answered "Here!" to the table, and the guard stepped aside to let him pass.

Here was my chance. I waited another five minutes, looked at the table, confirmed that everyone was busy, stepped up to the yard exit, and called out "Here!" The guard stepped aside, keeping his eyes on the prisoners in the yard, and let me pass.

No one was expecting me at the table, so I walked past it to the rear of the stage. Sure enough, there was the bathroom door, and I pushed down the handle. Paul had seen me straight—it opened, and I found myself facing a medium-sized window. I climbed over some cartons and opened it. So far, so good. I pulled myself up to the windowsill, sat there for a moment, and dropped down into the yard.

Once on the ground, breathing that warm, beautiful air of freedom, I pulled the knife from my pocket, opened it, and threw myself over a low fence into a neighboring yard. This was my lucky day—the back door was open, so I didn't have to force my way in.

I heard voices coming from the living room, but I didn't see anyone. I strode quickly down the hallway to the front door. "For your own sake," my inner voice told them, "stay where you are and don't come near me, because I'm ready to use my knife." It took me only a few seconds to reach the main door.

I was out on the street so quickly they wouldn't have had time to react. I folded my knife, put it back in my pocket, and turned quickly onto the boulevard, which had a tramline. It didn't take long for the next car to come by. Luckily, I still had a little money, enough for a fare. Changing streetcars at the Central Station, I arrived at my flat in the western district an hour later.

Once in my room, I realized how much strain the last ten days had placed on me—the constant vigilance and the planning for an escape hadn't allowed me much sleep. It was wonderful to be free again, but now that I was, and could start to unwind, I was exhausted.

I locked the door, undressed, and toppled into bed.

6

Another Border Crossing

I T MUST HAVE been 24 hours later that I woke up to a loud knock at the door: "Heinz, let me in." It was my trusted friend Ludwig. He'd had to quit his job at the toy factory right after my arrest. When I let him in, he chewed me out for taking ten whole days to escape. He'd expected far better than that and had been desperately awaiting my return so that we could go off on new adventures. He told me he'd been so restless that he decided one day to hang around outside the prison. He soon roused the suspicion of one of the guards, who checked his ID. Fortunately, it had passed inspection.

"So Ludwig, what's up? I've had some sleep, I'm feeling a lot better. What's our next move?"

"I can tell you that our days in Amsterdam are numbered. Most young men are being drafted to labor camps in Germany. Stool pigeons are popping up wherever you look to cash in on the rewards the Gestapo is offering. It's the only way they can fill their stomachs. I did some groundwork with the Resistance while you were away, and they told me a whole new plan is opening up that could help people like us."

"What's the idea?"

"We've got complete cooperation now between our group, the Brigade Blanche in Belgium, and the French Resistance. There's a guy named Pierre who lives in Brussels and knows every inch of the Dutch–Belgian border. He can meet us on this side and take us to his home in Brussels, then on into France."

"Sounds good, Ludwig. But what's their pitch?"

"They see us as reliable, as proven survivors. They expect us to report for jobs at the new construction sites in northern France. The Germans are in a hurry to build their new weapons—the V-l and V-2 rockets. The contractors are hiring everybody they can lay their hands on."

Then he added, with a twisted smile: "They also want us to use our German-language skills to find out what the new weapons program is about. On top of that, they expect us to travel between Holland, Belgium, and France to recruit 'laborers,' who are badly needed on the rocket pads. They'll supply us with lists, of course. In return, they'll provide us with perfect documents. For starters, both of us will receive authentic Dutch passports backed up by files at City Hall, where they've planted a few of our people by now."

"Ludwig, you've made my day. Getting out of here, an exciting assignment in a new country, French girls, good food and fresh air in the French countryside . . . What more could we ask for? Let's go for it."

"Okay. Let me set up a final meeting."

"Do that. Meantime, I'll get some groceries. I'm going to be starving. And I have to show my face downstairs to Mrs. Van Ruyven and Elly, and give them an explanation for my long absence."

With that, we parted. I walked the two blocks to the market, taking in every cubic inch of that beautiful air of freedom, did some shopping, and returned to my room, where I stuffed my face. Later in the evening, my landlords gave me a warm welcome. Elly played the piano for me while Mevrouw fed me cookies and tea, all the while giving me a long, puzzled look. Then finally she asked outright: "Jon, where have you been all this time?"

"Mevrouw, my job's been hectic the last two weeks. There was some traveling involved. You know how it is—I couldn't turn them down."

She was smart enough to know I was lying to protect her. Mainly, she was glad I was safe, and she wanted me to know that I could still trust her. Then I told them that I was likely going to be transferred to France but would try to keep my room if I could possibly afford it.

"Jan, don't worry about a thing. The room's yours, and we'll take care of the finance, as long as we possibly can."

Elly gave me a sad look, and I kissed her on the cheek. "Next time I'm back," I told her, "I'll take you to the Concertgebouw—it's a promise." That earned me a warm smile of platonic love.

The next morning, after another long, deep sleep, Ludwig picked me up and together we headed to the far side of the city to meet with some people in their apartment. I'd expected them to be a couple of thugs, but to my surprise Ludwig introduced me to a married couple about fifteen years our senior. A pair of soft-spoken intellectuals. The man addressed me:

"Heinz, congratulations on your escape from the Schouwburg. How were they treating you, how did you get out, and did anybody help you?"

I felt very comfortable with these people and didn't have the slightest doubt about their loyalty to the right course. So I gave them the clearest possible description of my internment there and made sure that Paul got his deserved plug. While I was talking, he was taking notes.

"Okay then. It seems they didn't break your spirit. You seem all charged up. Did Ludwig explain our plans for you?"

I told him yes, and he elaborated a little on what Ludwig had told me. He ended our meeting with these words:

"Pierre will be waiting for you this weekend at the border bus terminal. The line from there connects directly to the train station at Roosendaal. Exact time and day will be given to you the night before you leave, along with your itinerary. We'll have your new Dutch passport ready by then."

Smiling, he continued: "It takes us only one day, unlike the Germans—it takes them weeks with their bureaucracy. Now you have the pleasant task of picking a new name again. The Germans had you for ten days, so we don't want you to use the same name any more. Quick, let's invent you some new parents with their places and dates of birth, your new birthday and profession. And for God's sake, don't stop rehearsing them."

We decided that Ludwig would remain Willem Poppel, since he hadn't had any personal encounters under that name and was completely used to it by now.

I became Heinz Fenger, again with a German mother (but of a different maiden name).

When I looked them up, Hannes and Berta were ecstatic to see me again. They were already well informed about conditions in the Schouburg, my escape, the transports to Westerbork, and my future plans. Hannes, having saved so many lives by now, was well trusted by the Resistance.

They also told me that I was the only one who had escaped from the prison, though someone else had managed to flee at the train station. The sad news was that one of our leaders had been killed, a man who had always pledged that if cornered, he'd keep shooting as long as he had breath. He'd kept his promise. He'd been pointed out by a traitor, and when a Gestapo squad tried to arrest him, he killed two of them. The third body to fall to the ground was, unfortunately, his own.

The visit ended with another of Berta's home-cooked meals and some tears. We all knew we wouldn't see each other again for a long time and that we all had trying times ahead. But the news from the Russian Front was positive, and our determination to survive this war kept our spirits high.

All systems go. The next Friday morning, while the leaves were turning color on the outskirts of Amsterdam, Ludwig and I, dressed like Dutch laborers, headed south to new adventures in a fast and comfortable diesel train.

After five years as guests of Holland, where we'd quickly felt at home, it pained us to leave our friends behind. But we also knew we had to get out to save ourselves, and we were excited that we had a cause to serve.

After two hours, without any incident, the train stopped at Roosendaal. It would go on to Antwerp and Brussels, which was our destination. Unfortunately, we didn't have the papers to cross borders the easy way. Perhaps the next trip if everything went well, but for now we'd have to do it the hard and dangerous way.

The border station was lively. Porters were moving baggage around, passengers were making connections to other parts of the country. Uniformed Germans in military trains were making brief rest stops. This was on the Amsterdam-to-Paris main line. All the activity made us feel safer. We proceeded to the bus stop in front of the station without drawing any attention.

Our instructions were precise. The number and terminal of the bus to be boarded had been drilled into us. Photos of a variety of Belgian uniforms had been shown to us beforehand. This was a new country, and we had to know the difference between a policeman's uniform and a letter carrier's. We were standing in line with some other passengers, silent, mixing in easily. Everyone showed the burden of three-and-a-half years of occupation, with all the hardships that came with it.

The bus arrived. We paid our fare and looked for seats in the middle. That was the name of the game: never stand out for any reason, always look average and mingle with the crowd, and—most important of all—keep your mouth shut and stay low key. I'll tell you now: there would be times later on when loud-mouthed arrogance saved my life. More later.

We arrived at the terminus, less than a mile from the border, and everyone got off. There he was, easy to spot, just as described: smoking a pipe, wearing a gray cap and a white neckerchief, acting cool and confident—the impression of a nice guy, if you've ever seen one. We walked up to him and said, "Hello, Pierre." He nodded, gestured for us to follow him, and led us to a cafe around the corner.

We sat at a table and ordered some drinks, while Pierre gave us a close once-over. In a low voice, speaking Flemish, which is close to Dutch and which we understood easily, he said slowly, while pulling a daily paper from his side pocket: "Heinz and Willem, put your passports inside this newspaper."

We complied. Then he pulled the paper over to his side of the table, opened it, and slowly inspected our documents. After a minute, he folded the paper and shoved it back to us with a look of satisfaction.

"They look damn good," he said. "Who's the artist?"

"They're the real thing," I told him. "They'd better look good or the Dutch government will have to get themselves another printer."

"Okay. As you know, Dutch workers who volunteer for German construction jobs only need a valid passport and proof of employment on the contractor's stationery. Once you're in France, where I'll personally deliver you tomorrow, your passport will be enough, along with an oral declaration that you're on your way to an existing construction site. The place you're going needs workers badly. You just have to know your geography. Meantime, in about ten minutes I'll take you over the Belgian border. Just relax, like you're taking a Sunday stroll with me. The timing is perfect. I know which guards are on duty, and they know me and look the other way. Tonight you stay in my house in Brussels, tomorrow morning early we get on the Paris Express." He added with a smile: "Not all the way, though.

"Save your excitement for another time. We'll be leaving the train at Amiens, your passports are enough for the French border patrol. It's easier to travel from Belgium to France than from Holland to Belgium. I'll be leaving you in

Amiens and returning here while you connect with another train to Abbeville. There you'll find a bus in front of the station that will take you to Domleger. That was a farming village until six months ago. Then the Germans decided it would be an ideal site to launch their new rockets against England. They've thrown themselves into building it, you'll be amazed how lively the place is now. They hire any warm body that comes along for different phases of the work, they never have enough laborers. So if you know of anyone who has to run, just tell him to come to Domleger.

"Besides the workers—they're mostly French, and the others are from all over occupied Europe—you'll find German superintendents, a whole squadron of the Luftwaffe, a few sinister-looking guys walking around in long leather coats, who we suspect are Gestapo, and some nice French girls. Good pay and plenty of food. In the final stages of the project, we expect the SS to move in, and with all these Germans not used to being understood by their slaves, that's where you'll come in. So please, keep your eyes and ears open, we'll be asking questions. Tonight I'll supply you with a map, and point out your destination and transfer points as well as the train and bus schedules. Okay, let's go."

We left the cafe and walked through the narrow streets of this Dutch border village. It looked peaceful, and we reached a dense forest within minutes. Then we crossed an open meadow where cows were grazing, fenced in by barbwire. We went through the wire and came to a narrow strip of trees with a farmhouse on the other side.

"Welcome to Belgium," Pierre announced in his always-steady voice. "Another fifteen minutes and we catch our bus."

Back on a dirt road, a uniformed man on a bicycle was approaching from a distance. Pierre squinted for a moment, then reported with a smile: "That's Maurice, a friendly border guard. He sees no evil and hears no evil."

Sure enough, within minutes he'd passed us with a friendly "Dag."

We walked past more farmhouses, then reached a village. A bus was parked in a small market square, and we approached till we could read its destination: "Antwerpen."

We boarded, and little by little it filled up. The other passengers were mostly farmers. One of them gave Pierre a friendly nod. The rest of them examined Ludwig and me with puzzled looks. You just don't walk into a small farming village as a stranger without giving its inhabitants the satisfaction of identifying yourselves. Sorry folks, not this time.

The fields to our left and right were alive with harvest workers. We rolled along, making occasional stops, until the suburbs began to appear around us. More and more houses, some factories, then the first stores, and finally the railroad station.

Antwerp was a hectic place. For a few hours, we'd been able to imagine that life was normal. Now, in the big city, we were immediately reminded that the war was ongoing and that the Germans were still winning here in the west. Uniforms popped up here and there—the blue of the Luftwaffe, the green of the Wehrmacht, more women in uniforms than I had ever seen before, and, to my dismay, the hated double-lightning sleeve patch of the SS.

It was saddening to see another country dominated by these thugs, but by then I was also gaining confidence that we would beat them in the end. With a foolproof passport in my pocket and a cool hand leading us to the safety of his home, I was proud to have been accepted by the Resistance. I pledged to myself one more time that I would never let them down.

In the late afternoon we entered the chaotic bustle of the Antwerp train station. The city was a vital port and an important center for the diamond trade. The atmosphere became much more international as we boarded the express train for Brussels.

In Brussels we left the Gare du Nord, the main railroad station, and stepped out into the city's main square, which was overshadowed by a huge department store's neon sign: "Au bon marche." Trams were moving in all directions, and we could smell the exciting air of a metropolis.

Pierre pointed to a street packed with pedestrians. "That's our main shopping street. Let's walk a few blocks so you can get a first look at our capital."

It amazed us how much merchandise was still in the stores. We passed one window display after another. We also noticed that the prices were steep, though business was still brisk.

Pierre explained: "This city's become a legalized black market for occupied Europe. Money buys anything, and there's always someone willing and able to pay those prices, including the Germans."

We were especially attracted by the sidewalk cafes, where people were sipping good-smelling coffee and indulging themselves with pastries. Our mouths began watering—we felt like we'd landed on another planet.

Pierre pointed to shop windows filled with shoes, fashionable clothes, watches, jewelry, shortwave radios, and electric appliances. Then he turned to ask us: "When was the last time you saw all of that?" When we told him it had been a long time, he continued:

"While we're walking, let me give you some good advice. This city has plenty of informers working for the Gestapo. Some of them were arrested themselves and made a deal: they'd get to stay alive if they turned in members of the Resistance and other enemies of the Reich. The most dangerous informer is a guy named Jacques. He's on our hit list, but so far, unfortunately, he's still breathing. He looks very Jewish and has a keen eye for recognizing Jews on the run. He'll walk up to you all smiles and ask if you could help him hide, since he just escaped the Gestapo and is sure you're in the same boat. He's mastered several languages—sometimes he even comes up to you speaking Yiddish. He's always shadowed by his masters, and they're ready to close in as soon as he traps you."

We kept walking for a few more minutes while dusk settled over this lively city. The brisk autumn air felt good. Now we were reminded again that the war was still on: every shop owner was obeying the blackout regulations, and little by little the street began to dim.

As we turned the corner onto a boulevard lined with apartment blocks, we made the same observation: black paper drapes were being pulled down over the windows. The many bicycles and few automobiles and buses also had their lights covered, with a narrow slit across the center. Pierre led us to a tram stop, where we waited for our car with the other passengers, most of them French speakers.

We boarded the next tram and started to realize how big this city actually was. It took forty-five minutes for us to reach our stop in the suburbs. A few more minutes walking and Pierre pointed to a modest, well-kept private house. "Voila, my castle. That's where you'll be spending the night."

Pierre, we now learned, was a devoted husband and father. After he quickly introduced us to his wife and two children, dinner was served. The home-cooked meal tasted delicious, since we'd hardly eaten that day. After dinner, Pierre waved us into a small room, closed the door, and once more walked us through the following day.

Then he looked at his watch, nodded "just in time," and turned on a shortwave radio. "This is the BBC, London," we heard. "Today our bombers, escorted by Spitfires, raided . . ." A very familiar beginning to the recent British broadcasts. We sat in silence and listened. The news

81

was especially good that night. On the Eastern Front the Red Army was advancing rapidly, and to tie in with that, there was lots of talk about a second front and a landing in France, though no details were given.

The broadcast ended with a series of short, random sentences, delivered slowly and deliberately: "Rex gave birth to a litter of seven . . ." and so on. I had heard sentences like these before, but they had never meant anything to me. I watched Pierre's face react, sometimes with a smile. Later he told us: "Those were coded messages for the Resistance groups in occupied Europe, and for their agents, who are being parachuted behind the German lines. Get used to it—the day will come when some of those announcements are meant for you. Let's hit the sack."

7

FRANCE, 1943

"*Reveillez, reveillez*, wake up." Those were the first words I heard early the next morning. Pierre stuck his head into the room where we had slept the night, and after a little grumbling we followed his orders. We'd had a short, deep night's sleep, and now we were rushing to face another tense day.

An early-morning bus journey, the reverse of yesterday evening's, brought us through downtown Brussels to the Gare du Nord. It was much more peaceful there than it had been the afternoon before. After buying our tickets, we had just enough time to board the Paris Express, which was waiting to depart.

The south Belgian countryside passed quickly. After one stop at the border, we were in Lille, where the French border guards, supervised by the Germans, were pretty active. They entered our compartment, examined our documents, and looked satisfied when we told them our destination. Mainly, they wanted to know what we were carrying in our luggage.

They didn't have to spend much time on that: we were bringing a bare minimum. But I watched them open a large suitcase belonging to a woman across from us and go through it with a fine-tooth comb. I would learn later, to my profit, that there were plenty of ways to smuggle merchandise between Belgium and France.

We continued on to Amiens, where we stood on the platform and I hugged Pierre with tears in my eyes, bidding farewell to a man I had known for only twenty-four hours. It was like saying goodbye to a brother.

We moved to another platform, where we boarded a much older and slower train, which took us northwest almost to the English Channel, to the provincial town of Abbeville. Like clockwork after all the rehearsing, we found our bus on the market square for a forty-five minute ride to Domleger. That once sleepy village would soon be entering world history as a launching site for Hitler's "wonder weapons," the V-l and V-2 rockets.

It was mid-afternoon now. When we entered the village, we saw so many blue uniforms that we thought we were in a Luftwaffe base. We walked until we saw a fingerpost that declared "Arbeits Anmeldung." We followed it to a large barracks with a sign that said this is where we should register for work. A mild-mannered bureaucrat, a German, asked us, "Nationality?"

"Dutch," I told him.

"Both of you?"

"Yes," we answered.

"Any skills?" He looked us up and down.

"Yes," I said, "I'm an electrician, and my pal has done some carpentry."

"*Sehr gut.* You will be staying in Barrack 23 with other Dutch workers. Now go to the next room, where they'll place you on the payroll."

It was only appropriate that a Belgian employee, a master of languages, conducted the next phase. He looked at our registration cards and asked us in Flemish for our IDs. Satisfied with our passports, he gave me a puzzled look. "An electrician all the way from Amsterdam? Hell, you could find work anywhere."

"But not for the money you guys are paying here," I told him. "Besides, I like the French chicks."

No further questions, just completion of the paperwork. We looked at our pay scale and noted with satisfaction that, considering our free housing, even with heavy withholdings we'd had enough left over to eat well, and maybe even some spending money.

"Report tomorrow morning at seven at the platform under construction," the Belgian told us. "You'll see it as soon as you leave the village." He pointed through the window. "We can't assign you to your professions for the next few weeks because all hands have to help right now to complete a priority project—the pouring of the concrete bases. I think you guys will be good at weaving iron for the foundations. Your foreman will teach you anyway, and remember, feel free to put in all the overtime you want."

On the way to Barrack 23, we began to realize the huge scope of this project, which was rising in front of our eyes. On one side of the road were dozens of workers' barracks; on the other were almost as many—some of them still being built and much roomier. Those were being thrown together quickly for the Luftwaffe. Their trucks lined the lanes between their living quarters, parked neatly in assigned spaces. To my amazement, I saw that all of the larger vehicles had been converted to wood-burning energy, with large boilers mounted behind the driver's cab. The lack of gasoline must have been taking its toll, even at this base, which was so important to the Nazi war effort.

We entered our new living quarters and were greeted by a friendly guy from Rotterdam. "Welcome to the club. Where are you two from? I'm on duty today, cleaning the barrack. Why don't you take those two beds in the back? They just opened up."

We looked around the cramped quarters. About fifty people slept here in double bunks. There was a stove with a sizable grill on top. In the Dutch tradition, the space was meticulously clean. The beds had been made and all clothes had been stowed in lockers in between the beds.

"Let me tell you something," our new pal continued. "If you guys are on the ball, you can really eat well here.

Whatever you can't get on your ration card in the general store, you can pick up from the farmers around here at fair black-market prices. They don't realize yet what kind of money they can get for their bacon, eggs, and sausage in the big cities. So jump on it before they get wise to it. You can cook it right here on the stove."

A little later, everyone came back from work and the place filled up. They crowded into the washing facilities, which were in an annex next to our barrack. Then the stove became the center of attraction—almost everyone took his turn to prepare a small meal. The stores were closed by now, so we couldn't buy any groceries before the next day, but we found a good soul who let us borrow some bread and butter.

We slept our first night on hard mattresses we weren't used to. There was a nip in the air when we stepped outside the next morning. Winter was approaching, and we could taste salt in the breeze from the nearby coast. We walked a few minutes in anticipation of our new jobs, while workers swarmed in from all sides, reporting for their daily assignments. As we approached the construction site, we saw a man who seemed to be running the show.

He was obviously German, directing every arriving worker to his assignment for the day, and displayed a very pleasant attitude. We could sense the camaraderie between him and his crew. Most of the men approached him with the words, "Good morning, Emil," and he'd often answer with a wisecrack like, "What's so good about it," most often in German but sometimes in broken French.

This was a pleasant surprise for us. On a project this important, we'd expected the foreman to act like an obedient robot. When my turn came, I addressed him in German, telling him that we were new arrivals and were looking forward to working with him. He looked puzzled for a moment, and seemed relieved when I told him we were Dutch, not German. A few days later, I would find out why.

He pointed to an area a hundred feet away, where some men were carrying long iron rods and piling them in equally spaced places. "That stuff has to be laid out neatly and all attached together before they start pouring the concrete," he explained. "Have you ever done this kind of work?"

When we told him no, he continued. "There's nothing to it. Go over there, look it over, and I'll be there soon to start you off." He went on to direct the rest of the men to their different assignments, then came over to us with two more workers.

He pointed to one of them and said, "This is my best man. His name's Marceau. He'll teach you all the tricks of the trade. So, good luck."

Marceau, who only spoke French, began teaching us the proper distribution and layout of the iron rods and how to twist the soft wire around them to hold them in place. It wasn't all that difficult, except you had to get used to working bent over. We soon learned that Marceau wasn't just a good worker—he was also the most popular person on the site. Almost no one passed by without saying, "Bon jour, Marceau." The other workers looked up to him as their leader.

Our first working day passed uneventfully. We got used to our new environment and started to get friendly with some local farmers, from whom we would buy food supplies after our first payday.

Saturday night was the big get-together in the village's tavern. The place was jumping and always seemed to have enough booze on hand for everyone, even in this, the fourth year of the occupation. The first time we entered, some of the patrons had already drunk as much as they could handle. In the background we saw Emil with a pretty French girl, and Marceau, of course, was near them. They were already tipsy and started singing louder and louder.

Suddenly, Emil jumped onto a table to address the packed room: "Silence, everybody! I'm going to teach you a song and want you to fall in as soon as you grasp it. Here it comes: 'Volker hört die Signale . . .'"

I thought my hearing had failed me. It was the German version of the 'Internationale,' the Communist anthem, presented by a man trusted by his fascist government to supervise their most important project. This was in the autumn of 1943, at the same moment the Red Army was driving the German troops in bloody battles back to their Fatherland.

The crowd roared. Most of them hummed along, but some of them recognized the almost forgotten tune and sang along in French. Others just stood there in amazement, either not understanding what was happening or scanning the room (like me) to see if any SS or Gestapo were present.

When he finished the song, he topped it off by raising his fist and yelling at the top of his lungs: "Long live Ernst Thälmann." I didn't know how many people in the room recognized that name, but it certainly meant a lot to us. He'd been the head of the Communist Party in Germany, while working as a longshoreman in Hamburg, Emil's home city.

Thälmann had been arrested by the Nazis right after they took power in 1933. He'd been one of the very first prisoners in the Buchenwald concentration camp. Little did we know that he was still alive and that it would be my bad luck to join him there one year later.

These demonstrations were repeated every Saturday night, to our amazement. We all knew they would have to end abruptly sooner or later, and we hoped it would be as painless as possible for Emil's sake. Once he started to trust us, we were able to obtain a wealth of information from him, such as construction schedules and technical details of the launching pads.

One evening after our shift we came back to our barrack and gaped at who we saw waiting for us with his usual good-natured sneer: Leo, our poker partner during the long curfew nights in Amsterdam, had found a way to join us. We'd gone eighteen months without knowing what happened to him. We had dinner together and went for a long walk afterwards. He had always been a guy on the make, but the stories he told us that evening were incredible.

He'd turned into a master of escape. He told us that by now the Gestapo were having to resort to more and more temporary facilities to house their prisoners in Holland. After one arrest, they held him in a high school auditorium with scores of other prisoners, heavily guarded by stormtroopers. The very first night, he found a way for himself and ten others to escape through a skylight in the washroom.

Another time, he was taken into custody and loaded into a covered truck with two armed guards in the back of it. He made it his business to sit in the rear of the vehicle. At a slow curve, he shoved one of the guards off the truck and, quick as a rabbit, taking advantage of the confusion, jumped off and ran to safety.

His stories sounded like fairytales while he was telling them, but later on we got confirmation from a thankful ex-prisoner, at least for the first of them.

Leo was also a master electrician, with more field experience than I had. By then, electricians were badly needed on the building site. Barracks were springing up like mushrooms, and they all needed wiring. Our good relationship with Emil helped us get selected for that job. Leo and I formed a team to wire the place, with Ludwig busy doing our preparatory work, like drilling holes.

No one cared about safety regulations, since time was pressing. We pulled the hot feeder lines directly from the tops of the poles, sometimes over distances so that they were hanging low enough to be a danger to tall people. Even so, the work was pleasant and no one was supervising us. We were completely independent as long as we kept pace with the carpenters.

Some of the barracks were being occupied by the Luftwaffe before we finished the wiring. This gave us a chance to make friends with some of them and gather valuable information, which we passed on to our Resistance contacts.

I remember a short blond sergeant from Koenigsberg, a congenial guy who liked to have company while he was picking up materials from other towns with his truck. He took me along on several trips and even let me take the wheel at times. It was bizarre to be learning how to drive from a Luftwaffe sergeant.

Some evenings they invited us over to play chess. Other evenings we'd just sit around and talk about the war. I was always on my guard when some of them made hateful remarks about the Jews—remarks that had been instilled in them in the Hitler Youth. My little friend, the blond sergeant, never went along with that. "Our next-door neighbors were Jewish," he'd always tell them. "My parents and my brothers and sisters had a very good relationship with them as long as the law allowed us to. They were very decent people."

Statements like that, by him and others, led to what was a popular joke in those days: "'Germany had sixty million decent Jews. But how is that possible? All the Jews living in Germany, when Hitler took over, amounted only to 500,000.' 'Very simple, the German population was sixty million at that time, and everybody knew one good Jew.'"

We had a good life again. The work was pleasant, and we always had enough to eat, since we were on the best of terms by now with the local farmers—and also, for that matter, with their daughters. And best of all, thanks to my friend the sergeant, I had learned how to handle a truck like a pro. Our Resistance contacts didn't have any complaints either, since we kept them well supplied with information.

The unpleasant part was that security was growing tighter by the day. As the project neared wrap-up, more and more SS troops were arriving. Emil gradually calmed down until, one day, like that, he was gone. Had he been transferred to another job? Had his masters punished him for expressing his political views? No one knew.

One morning, while we were leaving our barrack for work, we saw a group of French workers holding an agitated conversation among themselves. Their eyes were glistening with anger and tears.

I walked up to one of them I knew and asked, "What's up?"

"Don't you know?" he almost sobbed. "Marceau was shot and killed during the night."

I was aghast. "How did *that* happen?"

"He was taking an evening stroll last night, feeling secure, because he was sure every guard knew him. Here comes this fucking SS rookie, maybe one day on the job, and screams, 'Password!' Marceau, in his usual way, answered, 'Come on, don't be silly, you know who I am.' Like *that*, the bastard pulls the trigger and Marceau hits the ground."

My French friend was crying now, and all I could do was join him. The news went around like wildfire—everyone was touched by it—and morale on the worksite fell to zero.

The German guards watched us carefully but didn't react in either direction (as was known to happen in other occupied countries). Then the commander announced there would be a funeral with full honors in the local chapel.

Domleger's only church was too small to hold all the mourners. Ludwig, Leo, and I went early to make sure we'd be able to sit inside. The coffin was placed on a pedestal in front of the altar, covered with wreaths. Many people could only watch from the street outside, through the doors that had been left open.

The French priest offered a eulogy for our friend, his eyes cold with anger. But he managed to control himself without hurling accusations. Our mood was rebellious; in this room where one of our comrades was getting his last respects, the fire in all of us was stirring. When we left the chapel, I pledged that I'd do what I had to do to avenge Marceau's needless death.

Christmas was approaching, and the war news was good. The Allies had defeated the Germans in Africa and had landed in Italy. Mussolini had been overthrown, which meant that the Axis was broken. The Russians were slowly retaking all the territory they had lost in the first part of the eastern campaign and were steamrolling toward Germany itself. Hopes were rising that the Allies would soon be landing in Europe to open a Western Front.

But the war was far from over. Hitler and his cronies were far from conceding defeat. In radio speeches, broadcast all over Europe, he declared that the Germans were developing a miracle weapon that any day now would destroy Germany's enemies. We in Domleger knew exactly what he was referring to, and we weren't at all certain the Allies would win in the end.

When we were allowed to take a short Christmas leave and see our loved ones in Holland, we jumped with both feet at the chance.

It was a pleasure to travel with a valid passport and a certificate of leave, all sealed and stamped by the local Wehrmacht headquarters. Studying this document gave us great ideas, which we would put to use soon after.

8

A CHRISTMAS LEAVE

C HRISTMAS IN AMSTERDAM was a delight. Hannes and Berta were still living in the same apartment on Rijn Straat, and they rolled out the red carpet for me. The city itself was quite somber. Most of the men had disappeared from the streets. They were working in Germany, or they had been arrested for political reasons. The short days and long curfews did nothing to cheer up the people. Food was getting scarce for the average citizen; the ration cards did not get them through the first week of the month, and the black-market prices were prohibitive.

Dr. Zubli, a devoted physician and patriot, was still going strong. He was still practicing, and he always found the time and the courage to help any fugitive who needed medical services. I went to see him during this short break with an embarrassing ailment, which he promptly cured.

Mevrouw and Elly were thrilled to see me again. Elly was a young woman by now, not quite beautiful but very,

very smart. I was glad to be able to keep my promise and treat her to a holiday performance at the Concertgebouw, conducted by Willem Mengelberg.

Berta's cooking was outstanding, as usual. They knew people in the right places who could supply them with groceries, and I never turned down any of her dinner invitations.

On my third day of vacation, when I entered their apartment, Berta said, "Heinz, I've got a surprise for you. Look in the living room."

I did, and I almost fainted. There was a bear of a man in the hated green uniform of the German military police. But my second look drew a broad smile from him. He approached me with a strong handshake and asked, "How are you, Heinz?"

Then I looked into the other corner of the room, and there was the *real* surprise: my nephew Dieter, now nine years old, was sitting on Hannes's lap. I was too overwhelmed to speak. When I finally got a grip on myself, I opened my arms just in time for little Dieter to run into them.

"Uncle Heinz, Uncle Heinz," he was yelling at the top of his lungs. I picked him up and we hugged each other silly.

Captain Reinmann looked on with a broad smile. "I'm Julius and Irma's neighbor in Essen," he explained. "You don't know me, but I've heard a lot about you and your cousins here. I came back from the Russian Front for Christmas leave and talked to Julius. Before I turned around, he came up with the brilliant idea that I should visit you guys in Amsterdam for a few days and take little Dieter along. I'd never been to Holland before, so it was tempting. I know the dangers, with Dieter being half Jewish, but then I figured that I'm safe enough in this uniform, and the damned war will be over soon anyway—believe me, I know, I just came from the Russian Front. The Red Army is chasing us, and with any luck I won't have to go back there."

By now my guard was up and I was watching him cautiously, trying to decide how to react. With gratitude? With sympathy? This was an army cop, trusted by his Nazi leaders to do clean-up work in Russia.

It was the blue-uniformed police who handled law enforcement in Germany. But this guy was wearing green, which meant he conducted special missions, like guarding prisoner transports, conducting border checks, and handling security in the occupied countries. The military police were older and more experienced than most of the SS troops, and in dealing with them, I was never certain which of the two forces was less evil. The SS men behaved like impulsive fanatics; the military police were more seasoned and calculating and killed with patience and precision. I tried to avoid the latter, so sure I was that they'd find me out faster than the SS.

It was decision time. I could stand there and spit in Captain Reinmann's face and tell him his hands still smelled of innocent blood, or I could be amiable, enjoy my nephew's visit, and pry as much information out of the captain as possible.

You guessed it, I decided for the latter. Common sense, and possibly my general optimism, helped me decide. I knew I was in for some strange moments—rare ones for anybody in my position at that time. Also, this man had lost half his loyalty to his cause already, and I welcomed the chance to tell him all about what the war was doing to civilians.

Dinner was served, and everyone enjoyed Cousin Berta's feast. The captain had slipped into civilian clothes and was feeling no pain after a few drinks. At first we made small talk about the war, and then it happened: he came around.

"You people wouldn't believe what's happening in Russia and Poland. I'm actually not allowed to talk about it, but what the hell, we've lost the war anyway. Human lives don't mean much anymore. At the beginning of our campaign, we followed our combat troops and treated the people in the conquered territories mercilessly. We punished the slightest resistance harshly, and many heads rolled. Now we're getting paid back in full. The Russians are moving steadily westward, destroying everything in their way. In my battalion, the list of casualties is longer than the list of survivors, and many of the poor devils who made it out have lost an arm or a leg. I'm counting my blessings to be with you lovely people tonight, still in one piece. The past year has changed my attitude so much that I'll never be the same again after the war. I only hope I won't have to pay for the mistakes I made in the early part of the war under strict orders."

He lifted his glass, took a big gulp, and looked at us with a glassy stare, as if he was yearning for our forgiveness.

The next few days saw the three of us riding the trams while I showed him the city. We went to the Rijksmuseum, the zoo, the harbor, and some other places I thought would interest my guests.

The captain took it all in in his green uniform, and little Dieter howled with excitement at all the new sights. All the while, I was glancing around, making sure I wasn't targeted by the Resistance for being seen with them.

Ludwig spent his leave with his own family and friends, and we didn't see each other for a few days. The last evening before our return to France, he came over and handed me an envelope.

"Here's your *Marschbefehl* for tomorrow morning. Both of us will be on the Paris Express. Our new assignment is in Paris—sounds like lots of fun. By the way, we have to take a few guys along over the French border. We meet them tomorrow morning at the station. They're listed as construction workers, cleared and stamped by the German authorities."

This was the beginning of 1944, and by now our people were planted in all the Germans' offices, so nothing surprised me anymore. After an optimistic farewell from my relatives, I made my rendezvous the next morning at the Central Station, full of confidence, with an authentic Dutch passport in my pocket. Little did I know that the worst was yet to come.

A list with the names of the "workers" was handed to me by a tall man in a raincoat who suddenly appeared and just as quickly vanished again. I looked the list over and glanced at the faces of half a dozen of my followers. To me they looked like a convict gang. Some of them had their heads down for fear of being recognized, and others looked tough and fearless. I'd been elected their guide across the two borders and had been assured that all their personal IDs were in order. Once in France, they would be on their own and Ludwig and I would proceed to Paris.

Our train was on schedule. We traveled together in one of the special cars reserved for the Wehrmacht and their emissaries. This was always the safest place, as long as you had good documents.

The first checkpoint at Roosendaal went smoothly enough. The station was swarming with German border guards both in uniform and in plainclothes. Most of them concentrated on the regular cars. Only two military police came to ours. I gave them the big welcome in German.

"I'm bringing construction workers over to northern France for our war effort," I told them.

"Die Liste, bitte!"

I handed him the transport list. After a glance, he returned it to me with a grunt of satisfaction. All this time, my guys followed their instructions, keeping a low profile and speaking only when spoken to. Ludwig, of course, acted as my assistant.

The second border crossing, in Lille, was almost a repetition of the Dutch scene, except we faced some extra questions about the contents of our luggage. This was to be expected, since Belgium had stocks of consumer goods that were in high demand in France and that could be sold at a handsome profit.

To my amazement, there was no search of luggage or garments; the guards settled for our answers. Clearly, it was an advantage to travel in a Wehrmacht car.

Our troop left us in high spirits at Amiens to proceed to the construction site in Domleger, which we had left only two weeks ago. Ludwig and I stayed on the train. A mission awaited us in Paris.

9

The French Resistance

THE EXPRESS TRAIN puffed its way through the long winter night. Sometimes I heard its whistle, while my neighbors dozed off. We must have been halfway to Paris when the train suddenly halted. Commanding voices were shouting: "Alles raus!"

As we dashed from our compartment we were ordered outside into the pitch-dark night. That's when we understood why. Searchlights were piercing the sky.

"Out into the field! All of you! Away from the train and duck!"

Moments later the air filled with the roar of the Lancaster and Spitfire engines. The Royal Air Force was on a night mission. The anti-aircraft guns, placed some distance away, went into action while I lay flat on my stomach and watched the show.

The engineer had been warned in time to stop before the RAF pilots spotted us—we surely would have been a welcome target. I marked up their lack of interest in our train to the fact that we were on a south–north run, while the Lancasters were heading for the Ruhr, due east.

A few minutes later, sirens in the distance blasted "All Clear." My heart was with the pilots and bomber crews in the sky. Good hunting and a safe return, boys.

We boarded the train again and continued on without incident, arriving in Paris on a gray winter morning. The Gare du Nord was packed, German uniforms of all kinds could be seen. Military police with their chest plaques controlled the scene, busily checking the military passengers of the many trains arriving and departing from this important terminal.

Cold-eyed men in long, gray leather coats, some of them wearing black boots, were scouring the crowds for fugitives. They needed no introduction—it was written all over their faces: "Gestapo."

And all the while, Frenchmen in berets were moving along, minding their own business.

Ludwig and I left the station quickly and boarded the Metro. This was a first underground journey in our lives, and we were excited about it. The sleek train moved underground at high speed, carrying us to our destination within minutes. We noticed that the cars had two different colors and decided to travel in one of the attractive red cars. The smell of perfume was overwhelming, and we learned as soon as the conductor checked our tickets that we had boarded first class and would have to pay a surcharge. We'd never repeat that mistake—even if you were colorblind, the smell of perfume would tell you right away you were in the wrong car.

We'd been advised to check into a cheap hotel in the Pigalle district, and after a little shopping around found a place that was reasonably priced and fairly clean. The concierge was suspicious of two young men who didn't speak his language well and who claimed to be Dutch. *C'est la guerre.* We were getting it from both sides of the political divide.

Our hotel was in a lively part of the city. The surrounding streets were a microcosm of Parisian life, though somewhat diluted by the three-and-a-half years of occupation. Curbside artists took shelter from the cold in doorways. The sidewalk cafes and flower kiosks were covered at this time of year, but we could tell how colorful the street would be in good weather.

We indulged ourselves for the first few days in this new and exciting city. After registering with the Prefecture of Police, we received our ration stamps and were able to purchase those long French baguettes. There was hardly any butter, though—the monthly ration was a fifty grams, just enough for two days.

The Resistance group gave us a week to poke around this wonderful city without any assignments. We took advantage, visiting the most important sights—the Eiffel Tower, the Place de la Concorde, the Louvre, Napoleon's

Tomb in Les Invalides, the Arc de Triomphe. We'd never seen architectural miracles like this. For two people as young as us, they were overwhelming.

The opera house was beautiful, but that beauty was diminished by its neighbor across the street—the German military headquarters for all of France, a reminder that the war was still on and that France was still an occupied country.

It didn't interfere with our pleasure that week. After a day of sightseeing, we'd spend the night visiting Paris's famous nightspots—the Moulin Rouge, the Montmartre cabarets with their naked chorus girls, and dancehalls where the bands played American jazz.

We were living it up, almost forgetting our precarious position and the suffering of millions of people all over the globe caused by this terrible war. All good things come to an end, and after a week, duty called again.

Late one evening after a good night on the town, I returned to my hotel room and found a young, clean-cut man waiting for me with a look that mixed congeniality with authority. "Bon soir, Heinz," he said in slow French. "Are you enjoying Paris so far?"

"Very much," I told him. "Who are you? Something tells me you have a message."

"My name is Michel, and I'll be your contact in the *maquis*. Feel like doing a little work with us? But before you start, let me make sure you're dressed properly."

He pulled a Luger out of his coat pocket and placed it on the table in front of me.

"Any experience a toy like that?"

"Nope."

"I didn't think so. Be ready tomorrow morning at eight. Roger will pick you up and take you to a special 'classroom.' Get some sleep now and make sure you rise and shine on time tomorrow."

With that, he left.

I sat there with my new gun, carefully examining it. There were no bullets, and I assumed I would get my supply with my lesson the next morning. Overwhelmed, I went to bed and tried to sleep.

Right at eight the next morning, there was a knock on the door. "Heinz, let's go. We have a lot of work to do."

Down the street, a black Citroen was waiting for me, occupied by three other guys. The rear door opened and I heard the words, "Come on, Heinz, join us."

Once I climbed in, the guy next to me introduced himself. "I'm Michel, and I've taken the job of making a good shot out of you within a few weeks, so they can rely on you for assignments."

We drove across town to a neighborhood I didn't recognize and stopped suddenly in front of a low-rise apartment house. Three of us left the car, the driver went on. I'd learn later that all of our cars were kept for only a few days and were constantly on the move for various assignments. Then they were dumped at any random corner and replaced by our own expert car thieves.

We climbed to the third floor and were admitted to one of the apartments, after Michel made a special knock on the door.

"Bon jour, mes amis," said the wild-looking guy who let us in. "Join the group. Now let's start our lesson. All of you've got your Lugers? Now I'll show you the wonderful things you can do with this little toy. I want you to become as familiar with your new companions as you are with your girlfriends. You'll sleep with them, eat with them, they'll be constantly by your side, and you'll learn how to use them on the spur of the moment."

He looked around the room, putting his own gun on a large table, addressing the earlier arrivals and us.

"Watch closely and count!"

Within a minute, he had taken his weapon completely apart and assembled it again.

"Don't be nervous—I don't expect you to do that as quickly this week. Now let's do the whole thing all over again in slow motion."

Slowly and deliberately he repeated the process, pointing out all the parts, calling them by their proper names, and indicating the lubrication points.

"Now try it with your own weapons, I'll give you some practice time. Ask me any questions you like, and when you feel confident, I'll supply you with ammunition, enough to kill a battalion of Germans."

After playing with my new toy for an hour, Michel walked over to me and asked, "Feel like trying it out to get the hang of it?"

"Why not."

He rounded up two other guys, picked up the phone, and said, "Let's go, our limousine is on its way."

We walked downstairs, where another black Citroen picked us up within minutes. It took us on a much longer ride this time, and I saw that we were heading west out of Paris. We entered a large forest, where Michel announced, "Le Bois de Boulogne, our hunting ground. So far the enemy hasn't touched it yet."

We traveled a few minutes to a remote area, where the driver pulled over. Michel took a dummy out of the trunk, walked to a small hill, and posted it upright.

"Voila, mes amis. Pull out your cannons, load them, and have fun."

Three eager guys, including me, jumped at the opportunity, feverishly getting our weapons ready, and started shooting away at the dummy. The kickback of my gun wasn't quite as bad as I expected, since I'd started out holding it with two hands. I was amazed how steady and relaxed I became in a very short time. I had to admit this was fun, and satisfying in a big way.

"Looks like I've got myself a good bunch of students," Michel said. "You guys will be ready for action soon. Now let's get back to the city."

He walked toward the road and let out a loud whistle. Moments later, our car returned to pick us up, along with the bullet-shredded dummy. I realized now that the driver had been covering us all this time, ready with a submachine gun to help us defend ourselves. All Resistance groups carried one just in case.

Back at the hotel, I ran into Ludwig again, and we decided to spend another night in Montmartre, checking out the nightclubs and eyeing the streetwalkers. We exchanged impressions of the day, and I learned that he had a different assignment than mine, related more to espionage than to gunplay.

Three nights later, after two more practice sessions in the forest, the night porter of the hotel knocked on my door at one a.m.:, "Monsieur Henri, you are wanted on the phone."

Half asleep, I walked down to the lobby to answer.

"Heinz, this is Michel. Answer only yes or no, if you have to. We think you're up to a special mission tomorrow morning. Dress casual, and be outside your hotel at nine. More details in the morning. Have a pleasant sleep."

My heart was pounding as I climbed the stairs back to my room. This was it—my first test as a Resistance fighter. How would I handle myself? Would I stay cool? Would I remember all I'd been taught? Would I be able to pull the trigger if I had to? That is, look someone in the eye and do that? And, most important, would my luck hold again?

All those thoughts were churning through my mind while I lay in bed and stared at the dark ceiling. Then I turned on the light again, reached under my pillow, retrieved my gun, checked the ammunition, went through a few motions of defense and attack with it, put it back again, and tried to sleep.

One of the requirements in our organization was to *always* be on time—that is, never too late and never too early. Either could increase the danger for the waiting party. That's why we took every opportunity to synchronize our watches.

The next morning I showed my face outside the hotel right on time. A moment later a guy who looked like an average Parisian, wearing a beret, walked up and addressed me.

"Heinz, follow me around the corner."

A Citroen was waiting two blocks away. Clearly, the driver wanted to avoid being seen by any neighbors more than once at the same pickup point, since by this stage of the war cars were available only to the privileged.

Three other men I'd never seen before were waiting in the car already. We drove off as soon as I joined them. This time the driver was moving faster than I had experienced before, waiting impatiently for the traffic lights to change. We arrived at our destination soon after, on a side street in a commercial neighborhood.

I spotted three more cars spread over a city block, all of them filled with passengers. A guy loaded with energy approached our car and handed each of us a sheet of paper, on which was drawn what seemed to be the plan of a bank.

"Study this plan carefully," he said. "It's the layout of a German military purser's office. We've cased the joint for weeks, and we know they're loaded today. They're preparing to pay out the salaries of the German occupation forces in Paris this afternoon, but our people need it more. Their security is a joke—arms are kept in the back room. They don't expect anyone to hold up the invincible Wehrmacht. Look at your maps and you'll find your names exactly on the spots where I want you to stand, covering a 180-degree radius with your drawn guns. Keep your eyes open and shoot at anything that moves in front of you—except me, because I intend to do some loading and may pass right in front of you. Your car is second in line. Now follow the men in front of you." He pointed to a car half a block down the street.

"I'll start things rolling," he added. "We don't expect any problems. The people working in this office are older, and some of them are women. You can rely on your getaway cars. Leave the bank as soon as you hear my command and jump into any car pulling up in front, whether you came with it or not. Good Luck!"

He rushed over to the lead car and got in. As it pulled away, we followed close on its tail. A few blocks away, we came to a stop and saw the car in front unloading its passengers. Our leader, followed by his men, entered an office building with large windows. Then we got the signal to follow.

The plans we'd been given were precise. Once inside, I found my position easily. I stood there and pointed my gun at the two green-uniformed men in front of me.

By then, every worker in the office was standing with hands up. Meanwhile, our people kept coming in and stabilizing our position. We had absolutely everyone covered.

Our leader stepped forward, pressed his gun against the temple of an officer who looked like the head of the pack, and demanded: "Open your safe!"

Without hesitating, the man guided him to a back room, which I'd seen some of our people penetrating moments before. Before long, one of our men came out with the first bag. Obviously, the safe didn't have a time lock. More moneybags followed, and then, suddenly, we all heard a commotion on the street outside.

Some pedestrians must have spotted people with heir hands up through the picture window and were peering in enjoying the excitement. A minor detail overlooked by our leaders.

By then the first car had pulled up and loaded up with moneybags. Our leader came walking out backwards, pointing his gun with one hand, holding a bag in the other. "We're pulling out," he called to us.

I looked outside and saw a squad of gendarmes running up and emptying their guns at one of our cars.

Right away, one of us fired a machine-gun burst in their direction, yelling, "La resistance française!"

Our man had purposely shot high, to give them a warning. They threw themselves onto their stomachs, their guns still drawn, pretending they were still doing their duty. Our next car pulled up, the barrel of a submachine gun pointing out the window to pin them down.

The gendarmes got the message, and we jumped into the car without any more shots aimed at us. Our driver pulled away and floored it. When I looked around, I couldn't believe my eyes—my old friend Leo was sitting next to me. He'd also joined our group. While we gaped at each other, the driver ordered: "Whenever I stop the car, only one person gets out. Then he goes home by Metro."

By the time my turn came, I had made a date with Leo. I jumped out of the car and noticed as I walked away that it had taken a few bullet holes in the lower body. My luck was still holding out.

10

Paris in the Springtime

THE WAR NEWS continued to be good. The Russians had broken the siege of Leningrad, the Allied air offensive was crippling Germany's industrial capacity, and rumors of a second front in the west were growing louder. But here in occupied France there was still plenty of work to be done.

The Germans were getting nervous. By this point they suspected everyone and his uncle of being a spy or a *maqui*. We had to be on constant guard. Even so, our organization was functioning well. We had planted our members everywhere. One very good-looking girl by the name of Lisa, born in Germany but of Jewish descent, managed to land a job in a Wehrmacht office as a secretary. I got to know her well, and my supply of blank, stamped German military documents soon became inexhaustible.

I was sent sometimes to Brussels to pick up small groups of "workers" for the German war effort. Each time,

I placed them in the military car of the Brussels–Paris Night Express. I always got away with it. The customs officers never examined any luggage—traveling with the German army provided a lot of immunity. The only problem was that I had to prove to the military police that I belonged in that car.

My documents had been adequate so far, but now, with Lisa supplying me, the sky was the limit. My financial situation became a little shaky, too, since Resistance fighters didn't enjoy the highest income bracket. Besides, there were some worldly goods I wanted to get my hands on, like a multispeed bicycle, a leather coat, a pair of long boots, a tailored suit, and a little spare cash for taking girls out.

It must have been that poem by Goethe that my parents had hung over my bed so long ago, which I translated now as "What Heinzchen wants, Heinzchen gets."

In my previous travels to Belgium, I had learned that people there were willing to pay top price for genuine French lipstick—in particular, *rouge baisser complet*. Now I had to research the Parisian market to find a product in high demand that was available in Belgium at a lower price. After a few days of chatting up merchants, I finally found the answer: batteries.

After weighing the pros and cons, I concluded that batteries were my best bet, in spite of their weight. I didn't have to lose on the currency exchange—merchants in Paris were standing in line to buy them from me, and the mark-up was fantastic.

There was one more link to make, and that's where my friend Lisa came in: documentation. At all checkpoints I'd have to be able to produce clean papers that entitled me to transport this kind of merchandise.

"No problem," Lisa said. "I'll have the documents for you by tomorrow. I'll make sure you could take the lipstick all the way to Berlin if you wanted. Just make sure you lose them in Brussels. The return trip will be easy—every German *Dienststelle* in France needs batteries. I'll even throw in some stamped blanks so you can tailor them yourself. Incidentally, you owe me dinner, now!"

Looking at her, I had an appetite already. "Anything you want, babe!"

My first black-market trip came sooner than expected. A day after I got my papers in order, Michel called me to let me know that four "workers" were waiting at the Gare du Nord in Brussels for the next night express to Paris. That gave me a few hours to shop for my merchandise in the cosmetic wholesale district of Paris. To match my luggage with that of the workers I was bringing in, I bought two large, cheap suitcases. Before leaving, I filled them with *rouge baisser complet,* which I purchased from the lowest bidder. That same night I boarded the express, which brought me to Brussels at six in the morning. The trip had been smooth. I had chatted for a while with a Wehrmacht sergeant who was sitting next to me. He had just returned from the Eastern Front and was very depressed and war weary.

"I can't tell you how bad things are over there. Half my battalion got wiped out. I'm one of the few coming back with all my arms and legs. The SS is killing every civilian they can lay their hands on. On the retreat, everyone we meet is labeled an enemy of the Reich. I've had it. I only hope the war will be over soon, one way or the other."

At the border, my papers were waved through, and no one even looked at my luggage. I was able to catch a little sleep for the rest of the trip.

I had to kill a few more hours until the downtown Bon Marché opened. Once it did, I'd be able to unload all my lipstick. By that point in the war, even reputable shops were working the black market. They were hungry for merchandise, and I had some.

I bought a newspaper, only to find that it was being censored and was reporting the same grand lie as in Paris: that the Germans were winning on all fronts. Then I went for breakfast in one of the many restaurants near the station.

The day went as planned. The department store swooped up my goods, paying in cash, and I went off to shop for batteries. Two suitcases of them made for a heavier load than before. I returned to the station, where I checked them at the luggage counter. Again, there was plenty of time to meet my gang. With the fast profits made today, I was toying with the idea of splurging on a black-market pastry. I picked a café nearby, which by that time of year had sidewalk tables. It had good coffee, too, to keep me awake for another night on the train.

So there I was, relaxing on a patio in front of the station, enjoying my snack, when suddenly about ten German military trucks pulled up. Soldiers poured out of them and quickly formed a picket around the square. After I got over the shock, I started to evaluate my situation. I was hemmed in, all right, but why were they doing this? I had full confidence in my papers, that wasn't a problem. But what if they were here to round up young men (like me) for war production in Germany? I was in no position to find out the hard way—at best, I'd be released after hours of interrogation and bureaucracy.

I had to move quickly before they finished setting up. So I paid my check and looked around for the officer in charge. There he was, a stocky lieutenant with medals dangling from his chest, busy screaming orders at his troops to form a perfect circle. Hundreds of people were trapped in this busy square, and it could take a long time to screen them all.

Without hesitation, I walked up to him and addressed him in my best German—

"Herr Lieutenant, I must congratulate you for your command of this raid. I just hope you catch some of those damned terrorists who keep us all awake. But listen—I'm on an important mission and have to catch a train immediately. So I hope you don't mind that I leave you to your duty. *Auf Wiedersehen.*"

With that I passed to the outside of the circle. He waved a friendly goodbye and returned to his mission.

The strain of four years of occupation was showing on the faces of my protégés, when I met them later that afternoon. They hadn't been eating well, and the strain of being constantly on the run was aging them quickly. Three guys and a girl made up this little group. The girl was wearing a green ribbon in her hair, her identification mark. Our introduction was short and to the point. I told them all how to behave and how to answer questions at the checkpoints. Soon after that, our train rolled in. By then I had examined their papers, which were clean. We entered the German military compartment to select our seats.

I had brought my two suitcases with me and now slid them into the overhead carrier. Night had fallen, and we were the first passengers in the car. Soon enough, all the racks and most of the floor would be cluttered with luggage and packs.

The train pulled out into the early spring night. There was time to relax before the next stop, which would be the border checkpoint. As usual, there wasn't any conversation among us. I took the opportunity to think about my place in the world. Would I ever see my parents, my sister, my dear friends again? The chances weren't good, if I went by the eyewitness information I'd been gathering from other travelers on my last few trips. The deeper I fell into my thoughts, the more determined I grew to keep the banner raised. I had been lucky so far, having survived two years on the Gestapo's wanted list. Luck and initiative had preserved me so far. So I must count my blessings, keep my cool, and live up to my obligations. The political and military news told me the war couldn't last much longer.

The train stopped suddenly, jerking our car and interrupting my reverie. All the lights snapped on, and a big German military policeman entered.

"Border patrol, Ausweise bitte."

Looking at us, he continued, "Aha, zivilisten."

Before he could ask any questions, I got up and handed over my papers. Knowing his rank, I addressed him with respect: "Gruppenführer Heinz Fenger directing four skilled workers to this construction site in France, Herr Unteroffizier."

With that, I pointed at the destination written on our documents, on which Lisa had done a superb job.

The guy had just started to check this train, and he probably had a lot of work ahead of him, some of it not so clear-cut. I knew that even in the disciplined German army, at this stage of the war, apathy was beginning to take hold. Some soldiers were overstaying their leaves a day, others were taking a little detour to visit a friend, so this border routine could take a little longer than it used to.

I hoped all of that was on his mind. In the end, he just compared our photos with our faces and sent us on our way, nodding "Sehr Gut."

This time I had to escort my people all the way to Paris. More and more Resistance fighters were needed in the capital as the invasion rumors grew louder. A second set of documents I was carrying made this possible. My business dealings also went smoothly. The enormous profits I was making on these round trips encouraged me to repeat them once a week for a short time.

My overconfidence almost led to a disaster, which made me call it quits, fortunately after I had made a killing on the black market.

I had heard about a train that shuttled between Paris and Berlin once a week, strictly for the German armed forces and their emissaries. It made no stops except in Brussels, Antwerp, and a few cities in Germany, nor were there any border checks. That train was much faster than the regular one between Paris and Brussels, but you had to prove you were entitled to ride it.

With Lisa's help, I tackled that problem too, this one supposedly small. So, I boarded the Berlin Special in the very early morning hours with my two suitcases of lipstick "for the ladies in Berlin."

I didn't have any trouble, but I was sticking out like a sore thumb. Everyone else was in uniform—no civilians here except me. Meanwhile, the stories I heard from the soldiers around me were worth any extra dangers.

One pilot knew that the Luftwaffe was finished, since his squadron hadn't received any fuel for the past two weeks. All their Messerschmitts were armed and ready, sitting in a field waiting for fuel.

An enlisted man in his forties was on his way to replace an SS guard in a concentration camp.

This was a rare chance to take the pulse of the German fighting men. Soon enough, I reached the happy conclusion that morale was plummeting.

The guys in London must have known about our train—that, or they happened to be flying over on their raids into Germany, which had became nonstop by now. The alerts and interruptions on that journey were the most I'd encountered on all my travels on that line. The train was almost hit several times, and the destruction of the tracks farther ahead forced a detour.

I left the train at Namur, a smaller Belgian city, to make a connection to Brussels. So there I was, with my two suitcases full of lipstick, walking along the half-deserted platform, trying to find the Brussels train.

The German officer who oversaw this station must have seen me as a chance to inject some excitement into his life. He came up to me from behind.

"Halt! Who are you and what are you carrying?"

"Wehrmacht goods, and here are my papers," I answered in arrogant German.

Examining my documents and looking at my luggage, he continued: "Seems in order, but a little unorthodox. I'm sorry, I have to call your office in France. Come with me."

He didn't look all that tough. I was certain that he just didn't have anything better to do and saw me as a way to impress his masters with his importance.

I made my mind up quickly. I'd brought in good money on these trips and knew you can't win them all. This guy was going to learn after a few telephone calls that the captain who had signed my orders didn't exist. My life was suddenly at stake, and so were the lives of the others in our group.

Luckily for me, he'd returned my papers to me for the time being. I followed him, carrying one suitcase while he took the other, and we made small talk until we arrived at a building at the end of the platform. During the walk, I told him about the "enemy" air raids on our train and how exhausted I was. He knew about it.

As soon as we entered the building, I put my luggage down and made a gesture like I was about to vomit. He pointed quickly to the restroom. I wasted no time locking the door behind me and making loud noises—which I hoped were appropriate at the time—then jumping through the window.

"I hope your wife enjoys the lipstick," I thought, "as long as you give me a good head start."

Luckily for me, again, most railroad stations in Europe were in the center of town. Once outside I was able to vanish into the crowds. Pretending to be a penniless Dutch worker—which was almost true at that moment—I hitched a ride south to a town near the French border. I knew that the next morning I'd be able to catch a Paris train from there, and I was gambling that he hadn't memorized my name and that even if he could describe me, a black market dealer would get low priority by this point in the war.

I checked into a hotel and assessed my situation, now that I was thirty miles from the captain. This had been a close call. But I still had my papers, and I was still in one piece. I could afford the financial hit, having enjoyed a few good weeks before now, so I'd be able to devote all my time to my organization from now on. Just let me get back next morning and forget this scare.

I boarded my train at dawn, feeling much better than the night before. One more tense moment at the border and I'd be home free. As I expected, I passed through easily and saw the Eiffel Tower in the distance by early afternoon.

I didn't do much for the rest of the day—just hung around in my hotel room, cleaning my Luger and catching up on the war news as presented in the censored papers. Suddenly I heard a loud hiss, as if some object was flying overhead at high speed. It was like nothing I'd heard before, and it had me scratching my head. Meanwhile, I heard a big commotion in the lobby downstairs.

Our building and the neighborhood didn't seem to be involved, so I got ready for bed. Just then, a knock on the door.

"Monsieur Henri, you are wanted on the telephone."

I rushed downstairs, picked up the horn, and heard Michel's familiar voice.

"Heinz, how are you?"

"I could be much worse. I'll explain later. Now I'm fine. What's up?"

"Did you hear that noise a little while ago?"

"Yes," I answered.

"That was the Germans finally launching their secret weapons against England. They're supposed to be some kind of rockets."

I knew he was calling from another public phone when he continued: "London is putting us on a crash program. The invasion is imminent and they want us to distribute their arms, which are being dropped in the French Alps and shipped by train to railroad stations in Paris, to different nests around the city. That seems to be the top priority right now. We've had some failures and lost some people here in Paris. The Germans are nosing around every corner."

Without giving me time to think, he added: "Incidentally, did you ever get the leather coat and boots you always wanted?"

I said I had. "They're wonderful. A long, light-gray coat and high black boots, if you didn't know me, you'd think I was Gestapo."

"I was counting on that," he said. "Wear them tomorrow morning. I'll pick you up at seven."

Punctual as always, Michel, accompanied by two nondescript Frenchmen, both wearing raincoats, entered my room in the morning.

Michel started in. "Here's the deal, Heinz. We have suitcases full of submachine guns, pistols, ammunition, and so on, direct from Grenoble, dropped by British and American planes. They're sitting in different railroad stations here in Paris. Our projection is that within a few weeks they'll be badly needed by our people, who are already waiting in designated positions. We'll be fighting shoulder to shoulder with the Allies as soon as the invasion has a foothold. Let me tell you, I've selected you for an important mission that could get you the Croix de Guerre. These two guys—" He pointed at his companions. "—are the best in the business with their guns. They're cool, and they don't miss. Trust them, please—they'll be your shadows for the next few hours, walking about fifty feet behind you. Of course, feel free to use your own gun if you have to. Your first stop will be the Gare de Lyon. Here are two claim checks. Present them at the luggage counter. The guy at the counter will hand you two medium-sized suitcases. You carry them onto the subway, following these directions, and deliver them at this apartment to someone who'll answer to the name François."

With that, he handed me another slip of paper containing precise travel instructions.

"Sounds easy? It isn't. You already know that all the Metro stations are guarded by the Milice Française, the Gestapo's best friends in this city. They're even more ruthless than their masters. They make you open up the smallest package, especially at all the entrances and exits of the Metro. Usually they've got two men flanking you. People like that are ass lickers when it comes to their bosses, when they aren't kicking their underlings. That's where you come in. Your job is to refuse to open your luggage by claiming to be a Gestapo agent.

"Play arrogant and insulted for being asked to open them. Use every German word to humiliate them, and delay opening the suitcases for as long as you can. The instant you fail, there'll be two dead bodies on the floor and plenty of time for you to run. Your two bodyguards will be right behind you, watching the show innocently, like any bystanders would. But each of them will be aiming at one of your interrogators with his weapon cocked in his raincoat pocket. So, go and enjoy yourself."

My two stone-faced comrades stared at me and nodded *let's go.* I left for the nearest Metro station.

The Gare de Lyon was easy to reach from my hotel. The first part was easy, and I practiced the authority I was going to have to display before the morning was over. The suitcases were handed to me without any hesitation. When I picked them up, I was taken aback how heavy there were. For a minute I thought about hiring a porter, but I rejected the idea immediately, remembering my oath of obedience: "Always carry out your orders to the letter, to protect your own life and those of your comrades."

I turned my head from time to time and saw my shadows following me faithfully. Then I walked carefully to another platform, where I waited for my train. Some characters were standing around looking at me, and I couldn't decide whether it was with hatred or respect. My confidence was growing by the minute. Even I almost believed I was a Gestapo agent going on leave to Germany. (Lisa had contributed to that impression by providing the proper documents.)

So far, so good. I approached my destination stop, knowing full well that no one carrying a package was going to reach street level without being searched. Slowly and deliberately, I walked up the stairs. One more glance behind me . . . There were my shadows. Sure enough, at the top of the stairs, two aggressive-looking Milice men were stopping everyone and demanding to inspect their packages.

Now, the moment of truth. I climbed to the top platform and walked right in between them.

"Sir, what is in your suitcases? Please open."

I put my luggage on the floor, cranked myself up myself to my full five feet eight inches, cocked my hands on my hips, and turned from one collaborator to the other with the most arrogant expression I could muster, screaming at the top of my lungs, "Das geht Euch einen Scheissdreck an!" Translation: That's none of your fucking business!

One of them looked stunned. The other one approached me with a simpering look.

"Vous êtes Allemand?"

"German, hell! I'm Gestapo!"

"We apologize, sir but please understand that we have to do our duty. Please continue, sir."

The *maquis* received my first arms shipment safe and sound. There were quite a few more to follow. Most important, our method worked every time and there was never any bloodshed.

11
D-DAY

B ECAUSE OF THE huge concentration of the forces in Paris and that city's importance as a transit center, the Germans placed all their offices off-limits to everyone except those in uniform or who were carrying proper ID.

There were movie theaters, shops, restaurants, even brothels strictly for the use of the Wehrmacht. Meanwhile, food was getting harder to come by, and black-market prices were spiraling. As for me, I could always enter a German restaurant by flashing my perfect ID and putting on an attitude of self-assured formality, like a German. A decent meal at a fair price was always available. Quite often, I met people in those places with interesting information to pass on to the Allies.

I even got up the nerve to date a *Blitzmädchen* freshly arrived from Germany for a few days' leave. *That* was exciting. The few times we met, our motto was: "Let's live it up tonight—we might be dead tomorrow." Luckily for both of us, she continued on to western France, where even the Germans now expected a second front to open soon.

Another time, I was having a meal with a Luftwaffe sergeant. He was intelligent, very well mannered, and pleasant company. We decided to see a movie together after dinner. We met a few more times after that and began to develop a friendship. After he got to know me a little better, he approached me one day—he wanted to desert and asked for my help..

"We've lost the war. My father has always been a known anti-fascist in Bad Godesberg. I don't feel secure with Nazis any more. They could fall on me at any moment and I want to fight the Nazis before it's too late. Can you help me, Heinz?"

I was shocked.

"Herman, I can't imagine why you're asking *me*. I'll just pretend I never heard you. But you're welcome to meet me again and tell me more about your troubles."

We set up another meeting time, and I went on my way—to call our group together for an urgent meeting. We all thought it over from every angle, then we came up with a plan.

"First," Michel decided, "let's see if he'll bring his uniform and some arms along. We'll promise him clothes, and room and board. The very first day we'll put him on a mission, to see if he's sincere and has nerve. Your friend Leo will be the leader—he's got enough experience.

"We have a list of French traitors and collaborators," he went on. "Most of them will get their punishment after the liberation, but some of them are especially dangerous and are hurting our cause every day. We can't allow them to live any longer—they have to be executed. We've made absolutely certain we're hitting the right people. It was a hard decision, but you have to trust us. For each one of them dead, we'll be saving a dozen of our own. Everyone on the execution team will be supplied with all our information about the crimes against France his target committed.

"Heinz, on your next meeting with Herman, you'll bring another man. Four eyes can see more than two. If he agrees to our conditions, he's in.

"About the execution teams, each will have one driver and three executioners. They'll all shoot at the same instant so that none of them knows who fired the lethal shot. All of this is strictly on a voluntary basis, except for Herman, who has to be blooded."

I met Herman on a street corner at the appointed time, with my companion covering us from a safe distance. I noticed nothing suspicious, so I took him for a long subway ride with my shadow within reach. Climbing the wrought-iron steps out of the last station, I recognized one of our cars idling at the curb. I jumped in the front beside the driver, and Herman behind me, and a moment later our shadow joined us beside him.

Herman was acting scared, which was natural and only added to my satisfactory impression. He just didn't have the aura of an agent, and he agreed to all our demands, though he hesitated before he said yes to executing a traitor. He promised to bring his uniform and two handguns. After setting a meeting place for the following day, we released him in the middle of nowhere.

That ended my personal involvement in Herman's desertion from the Luftwaffe.

I didn't volunteer for the execution team, but Leo did, and a few days later he told me all about how it went.

"There was this young guy, a highly active Gestapo agent, living with his mother. We knew the names of his contacts, and one of our men used them to get into his apartment early in the morning. Our car was a short distance away. The guy jumped when our own guy told him one of his superiors wanted to see him right away for an important mission. Mothers, though, have a sixth sense. She started making a scene, begging her son not to go with us. He calmed her down, telling her everything was under control, and walked downstairs with our guy. Our car picked them up immediately. We pushed him into the back seat and three of us held him down. During the ride to the Bois de Boulogne, we held a tribunal. We read out the names of all the people he'd turned over to the Gestapo, which resulted in their arrest and sometimes their execution. The sentence for his crime was death, to be carried out immediately. He tried to defend himself, of course, and gave us all sorts of excuses for his actions. When we got to the forest, we pushed him out of the car and shot him."

"Thanks, Leo. I'm glad I didn't have to be part of it, but I understand why it was necessary."

Air raid sirens were becoming more frequent by the day. The air was full of excitement for most, and fear for some in and around Paris. On June 5, 1944, sirens and all-clear signals were blasting constantly, but not one bomb was dropped on the city.

Our arms and ammunition had all been distributed to the resistance nests. We were ready. The next morning the German authorities broadcast a special bulletin—

"The Allies have made a landing attempt in Normandy. We have inflicted terrible casualties on them and are convinced that within twenty-four hours all their divisions will be eliminated. We are warning the population of France that any assistance to the enemy will be treated as a war crime and punished by death."

I made a point that night to have dinner in a German restaurant, where I listened to the different opinions of the enlisted men. To my surprise, I found that most of them believed their own military reports and were certain the invasion would fail. They even believed that Hitler was ready to launch his "miracle weapon" and destroy England within days.

I was taking every opportunity to listen to the BBC. From them I heard an entirely different story. The British sounded optimistic and were reporting that, in spite of some initial difficulties and casualties, the landing were going according to plan. Within a few days, they were broadcasting the names of liberated French villages.

Our missions were light at first. We planted ourselves on the main roads in and out of Paris and counted all the German troops and ordnance moving in either direction.

June 19, 1944, was a beautiful early summer day. I decided to spend a few hours at a public swimming pool. When I returned to the hotel, Michel and another man were waiting for me.

"Heinz, one of our men has disappeared with several handguns and a submachine gun. We don't know what his motive was, but we suspect it may have been monetary and we don't think he's a turncoat. We've got word that he's hanging out this afternoon in a tavern outside Paris. Both of you have to go there right now and persuade him to hand over the arms to you. He won't be punished. We're sure he's just harmless and frightened."

"Heinz, your job will be to sit in, mumble a few German words here and there, and open your coat sometimes to let him see your gun. Ernest will conduct the negotiation in his own language. By the way, the invasion is going well—we should be hearing the American Shermans within days. Good luck."

We took the Metro to its terminus and continued by bus to a small suburb. Our man was sitting at the bar, and he recognized my companion immediately. Surprised and frightened, he followed us to a table in the corner pointed out by Ernest. The plan worked well. He admitted what he'd done, apologized, and had us follow him to his apartment nearby. There he handed us a submachine gun and four pistols. I packed them carefully into my suitcase after disassembling the former. It was time to return to my hotel.

On leaving the Metro, I went through another luggage check, which I passed easily, Ernest shadowing me.

It was late when we arrived at my hotel near the Place de la République. Several members of our group had rented rooms in there, other in nearby hotels. We stowed the confiscated weapons casually in a closet and, as usual, I placed one handgun under my pillow, fully loaded. Ernest stayed with me. It didn't take long for us to fall fast asleep.

At three o'clock in the morning, there was a loud knock on the door. Half asleep, I called out: "Ou est la?"

"Herman!"

"What the hell do you want in the middle of the night?"

"I have to talk to you, Heinz, it's urgent, please let me in!"

He was a deserter, but I trusted him—by then, he'd proven himself a brave and reliable fighter for our cause. So I slipped on a pair of pants and dropped my Luger into my right pocket. Then I slowly opened the door . . . and stared into the barrel of a submachine gun pointed at me by a stranger. Herman was standing off to one side, with eleven more men, all Milice Française and fully armed—a tough-looking bunch. Herman had let himself be used as bait.

"Haut les mains!" the gunman demanded.

I sized them all up and concluded that this wasn't my time to die. I was close enough to take the first one but not the rest. I envisioned terrible days of torture ahead; on the other hand, the Allies were less than a hundred miles from Paris. So I raised my hands, as requested.

They handcuffed me to Ernest, then ransacked my room. The haul of weapons made them ecstatic. They slapped one another on the back, then cuffed my face when they found the gun in my pocket. Then they led us down the stairs to a row of five black Citroens in front of the hotel. I knew that make well by then. Unfortunately, they weren't ours.

They held Ernest and me at gunpoint against one of the cars. Herman started pointing out the other rooms in the neighborhood occupied by our group. Most of the *milice* busied themselves rounding us up and bringing us back to the cars, one by one and in handcuffs. By the end of the night, thirty-two of us had been arrested. I stared at all these familiar faces and wished for a moment that I'd pulled my gun back upstairs, so I wouldn't have to face this humiliation. I was blaming myself for introducing Herman to the rest of us.

Later on, I got conclusive evidence that Herman had been spotted by the German military police and arrested. He realized full well that he'd be shot within days for desertion during wartime. His knowledge of our group would save his life temporarily. So he cut a deal: his life and his freedom in return for everything he knew about us.

None of which made me feel any better.

I had time just then to observe our guards, and saw that they looked away from us every time a new arrival was delivered. Also, they became disorganized each time they loaded more prisoners and confiscated guns into the cars. I stared at Herman, who was still handcuffed to me, until he guessed what I was thinking. It would be a long and dangerous run to the next corner, but if there was any chance for us to escape, we'd have to exploit the guards' confusion.

A minute later, at the height of the excitement, I measured the distance to the only gun pointed our way, took a deep, silent breath, and kicked it into the air with my right foot. My soccer coach would have been proud of me.

Ernest caught on immediately, and we started running together. We had a good head start in the darkness when the first submachine gun burst sounded. Bullets were flying past us left and right from behind. We kept running in a zigzag. So far, so good. Then, just before we turned around the corner, I felt something sting and a warm liquid running down my right calf. I didn't know what exactly had happened and wasn't feeling any real pain, so we kept running till we reached a small apartment house a few blocks away. It was a blue-collar place, too small to have a concierge on duty, and the entryway was open. There were toilets on each landing.

We walked up one-and-a-half flights, entered one of them, turned on the light, and locked the door behind us.

Ernest was unhurt, but my calf was bleeding heavily and I could see where the bullet had struck me. We washed the wound. By that point I was starting to faint and the pain was beginning to take hold. I tore a strip from my shirt, and Ernest helped me apply it as a bandage. That was difficult, with the two of us handcuffed together. It was still early morning. We just had to be patient and wait for the chance to make our next move.

Around six o'clock, we heard the apartments begin to stir. We'd have to take our chances and ask one of the families for help, hoping they were still patriots. With Ernest, I limped up the steps and knocked on a door. The man who answered asked us a string of questions, then grudgingly lent us some tools. He even helped us remove the handcuffs. We thought we were home free now, as long as my strength held out long enough for us to reach one of our contacts in a different neighborhood.

While leaving the building, we walked right into the arms of the French police. The Gestapo had ordered them to comb the neighborhood for us.

"It was easy," an officer sneered, pointing to my leg. "All we had to do was follow your blood trail."

I looked around and noticed—a small mercy—that the arrest this time had been made by the French police. We could hope for more leniency from them than from their German counterparts. Two officers led us to a police

141

van parked in front of the building. They placed us in the driver's cab and made us wait while their colleagues finished combing the building in the hope of finding more escapees.

Armed police were flanking each side of the vehicle, very close to the unlocked doors. I glanced at Ernest, and he read my mind again. I slammed the door on my side open, knocking down the cop, and Ernest did the same. We had a few seconds to run to the next corner, and that's what we tried to do. Halfway there, I felt an unbearable pain in my wounded calf. I slowed down to a snail's pace and glanced behind me. The two officers were on their feet again and were aiming their guns at us in a braced position.

I told myself we couldn't expect them to save our lives and sacrifice their freedom after we'd just humiliated them. So once again, I raised my hands in surrender. A little way down the street, Ernest did the same, and I wondered why.

Needless to say, they didn't give us another chance to escape. Each of us was handcuffed to an officer and delivered to a nearby precinct house. Soon after that, two blond-haired, well-dressed civilians entered the room where we were held. No introduction required—this was the Gestapo.

"You swine, who the hell do you think you are, giving our people such a hard time? We know all about your crimes. The party's over and you're going to pay dearly."

With that, they handcuffed us again and pushed us out onto the street, where their car was waiting.

"Excuse me, sir," I told my guard. "I'm seriously wounded with a bullet in my leg. I can hardly walk and have lost a lot of blood."

He laughed out loud and slapped my face.

"You bastards don't have to worry about a bullet. We'll give you another one soon enough, and that'll cure you."

The car took us to the Place de la Madeleine, around the corner from the Gestapo headquarters for all of France. I'd heard a lot of gruesome stories about that building, and being hauled toward it myself was a nightmare.

Herman and I were separated, and I was taken to the private office of the Gestapo officer who had arrested me. The plaque on his desk read "Sturmbannführer Ritter." He planted himself in a comfortable armchair, opened a door, and produced a bottle of whisky and a whip, placing one on each side of his desk. Then he took a deep gulp straight from the bottle and started his interrogation.

"I heard that besides all the crimes you committed, you have some Jewish blood in you."

Someone must have spilled. I had enough troubles already, without having to get around that.

"No, Herr Sturmbannführer, that was a lie I told them so they'd trust me."

He gave me a glazed look and knocked back another mouthful of whisky.

"Drop your pants!"

I followed his orders.

"Aha . . . a Jewish penis, you damned liar."

With that, he swung his whip across my upper body. The pain was excruciating, and I didn't know how much more I'd be able to endure.

"Some more serious business. How many of our good people did you kill with that arsenal we found with you?"

"None, sir," I answered.

There came the whip again across my body. My tormentor took another gulp from his bottle.

"We're going to cut you swine down to size and make you confess if it's the last thing we do."

By now, I had only one wish: to lose consciousness before I had to answer more questions. But that wish wasn't granted to me yet. The interrogation went on like that for what seemed like eternity. Just when I was about to faint, he called in some underlings and the two of them dragged me down to a car.

"Is this it?" I wondered. "Am I going straight to a firing squad?"

It was a beautiful summer day. Paris looked lovely as we drove out to the suburbs. "Take it all in, Heinz," I told myself. "This may be your last pleasure." We turned into a large complex through a gate guarded by two German soldiers. This was the German armed forces hospital. They pulled up to a separate wing, one that had windows with iron bars. Then made me limp inside and introduced me to the officer at reception.

"This swine is extremely dangerous," the officer told him. "He escaped twice already. Keep him alive a little longer—we need to get more information out of him."

This was it—I was in the soup now. I told myself that the longer I could withhold information and endure the torture, the better a chance I would have to stay alive. Maybe long enough for the Allies to arrive and save me. It was worth trying, but did I have it in me to succeed?

To the good, I was in a hospital now, in a room of my own. By then my temperature was soaring dangerously. A young doctor from Vienna treated me and was quite humane about it. He followed his orders precisely, applying compresses on my leg and trying to work my temperature down.

While I was there, word leaked into my room that on July 20, 1944, at Wolfschanze in East Prussia, some of Hitler's senior commanders had made an attempt on his life. Perhaps the end was approaching and better people would take over the Reich and surrender to the Allies.

But Hitler had survived the attempt with only a few scratches. From that point on he would trust no one and turn against all. Meanwhile, the Gestapo had their hands full investigating even their own people. All of that, and the Allied advance toward Paris, could only help me.

My wound was healing quickly, even though they hadn't taken out the bullet, and I was recovering my strength. One day the door to my room flew open and I was staring into the eyes of my feared interrogator, Sturmbannführer Ritter. He looked drained and more nervous than the last time I met him, but his hatred for me was still written on his face.

"Get dressed and follow me. Your vacation's over. You're in for another party in my office."

Once again, he handcuffed me to himself and led me out of the building, where a car and driver were waiting. The ride back to the Place de la Madeleine was frustrating. I knew I had no hope left. He took me upstairs to his office immediately, and once again out came the whip and the bottle. But I also saw that the atmosphere in the room had changed. He was still arrogant but he was subdued about it, and I could see defeat in his eyes. But that didn't stop him from trying again to break me.

"I'm going to read you the names of some terrorists, and you're going to tell me everything you know about them. Remember, the more you spill, the better your chances I'll let you live."

He read off three names I knew very well, then looked me in the eye and added Ludwig's name.

"I've never heard of the first three," I told him, "but I know Ludwig. He was my roommate. I met him here in France, but we never worked together."

Down came the whip on my shoulders. As the interrogation went on, I fed my tormentor some fabricated information. He only bought some of it, and my tortured body began showing which parts of my statement he didn't believe.

Just before I collapsed, he called one of his hangmen in and commanded him, "Take this swine to Freignes."

I'd heard that name before, and the wheels began turning in my semiconscious mind. Then it came to me: Freignes was the prison near Paris where captured *maquis* were held and executed.

147

12
BUCHENWALD

FREIGNES WAS GUARDED by Wehrmacht troops, most of them too old to qualify for combat. While I was stripping off my clothes to change into prison garb, an officer looked me up and down and asked me where all those fresh marks on my back and shoulders came from. When I told him the truth, he started cursing—

"That's all the damned Gestapo is good for."

That was encouraging: a German soldier had found the nerve to condemn the Gestapo in front of a prisoner. Maybe it meant that my treatment here would be more humane.

Within a few days, I found out that *was* the case. The older guards were less fanatical and could see the handwriting on the wall. In fact, they became friendlier as the days passed, and I could tell from their faces and their conduct that the Allies were getting closer to Paris.

They supplied me with newspapers, books, and magazines, and the food was bearable. When they talked to me, they told me a little about themselves, always making sure I caught their name. Obviously, they were trying to establish alibis for after the war, when the victors would judge their treatment of prisoners.

Two uneventful weeks passed, long enough for me to strengthen myself for whatever came next. I knew I was a marked man and that my real enemy hadn't forgotten me.

Then, one morning early, there was loud and excited banging on all the cell doors: "Everyone up and prepare to move out." Once my cell was unlocked, I walked over to the transport registration desk. The officer asked me a few basic identity questions and then declared me eligible for the transport. No one told me where it was going. Soon after, enough prisoners had been processed to fill a bus. We boarded it under heavy guard and were driven to a railroad freight station in eastern Paris.

On arrival, we found out right away that our guards' humane treatment was over. About forty cattle cars were lining the station, coupled to two locomotives. Every third car had a raised compartment occupied by two SS guards, who aimed their machine guns in either direction.

The platform was crowded with SS men, some of them leading attack dogs and all of them heavily armed, screaming orders at the prisoners and shoving them hard into the cattle cars. When my turn came, I tried to get a place to sit near a window, but after a few minutes I had to get up because we were all being squeezed in like sardines. I counted seventy people in this one car. Later on, at rest stops, I confirmed that count with one of the other prisoners.

It took an eternity to load all the cars, and then the train just sat there. Doors were shoved open and names were called out. Moments later, I heard people screaming and then a burst of machine-gun fire. Clearly, the Gestapo had decided to conduct some last-minute executions, right on the station platform.

Would I be one of them? I pushed myself deep into a corner. No way was I going to answer if my name was called, and they'd have a hell of a time finding me in this jungle of prisoners. In any case, I knew they were anxious to get the train out of there. Even then, I could hear the rumble of tanks and artillery fire in the distance.

Finally, the train started to move. Through a crack in the wall, I saw three bodies lying on the platform.

The first few hours in the car were bearable. Many transports in those days were carrying families and old people. This one was packed with Resistance fighters, most of us young and strong. So there was a spirit of camaraderie. We tried to survive in the small area of the cattle car that was available to us, without stepping on one another's feet.

But by nightfall, human needs were calling. We were hungry and we had to use a bathroom. Fortunately, our guards sensed that just in time. They stopped the train in the countryside just before dusk and ripped open the doors: "Alles Raus."

I jumped down from the car with mixed feelings. I was glad of the chance to stretch my legs, breathe some fresh air, and take a leak. On the other hand, we were exposing ourselves to our SS guards, who were probably carrying lists of "criminals." This would be their chance to eliminate the ones they had labeled as no longer useful.

Whatever, I had no choice, and left the car with the others. As soon as I hit the fresh air, I had one thought on my mind: *Run.* Then I looked again, aghast at the number of green uniforms surrounding us. There had to be 1,000 SS men guarding 2,000 prisoners. That had to mean they were retreating from the Allies while they were guarding us. In no way would I be able to find a hole in that net.

They lined us up along the railroad tracks, where we formed an impromptu irrigation system. Some of us, of course, had to go deeper into the field, but machine guns were set up all around, manned by hardened Waffen SS troops.

When I looked around for familiar faces, I got a pleasant surprise: a hundred feet away I spotted Leo, my escape artist friend. Whatever it took, we had to join forces. I was sure that between the two of us, we'd be able to escape. Preferably on this side of the French border, but if necessary even in Germany, where we were undoubtedly going now.

The first step was quite easy. By now things were so tense and confused that nobody noticed when Leo joined us in our car. We had received some water and soup before, which had been hastily prepared in a field kitchen. So far, so good—we had survived that first stop. We weren't looking forward to standing for the whole long night ahead, but where there's life, there's hope.

The next twelve hours were horrible. Exhausted, I dozed off against someone's soft body. When I woke up, Leo gave me a questioning stare.

"So how are we gonna escape?" he asked.

"Right now, Leo, I couldn't tell you. Yesterday during the rest stop, I didn't see the smallest chink we could have squeezed through. There's just too many damned SS, all armed to their teeth. That might change today. We'll just have to see at the next rest stop."

"I agree with you, Heinz, but I haven't given up. Keep your eyes on me. When I start running, you follow!"

Another hour passed. Daylight was seeping into the car.

Suddenly we heard a loud roar overhead, followed by a tremendous explosion ahead of us. The train came to a shrieking halt, doors were slammed open, and the entire SS garrison took up positions around the train, weapons cocked. "Alles Raus!"

Outside, I saw to my delight that the tracks in front of us had been blown to pieces. A little beyond that, I saw a railroad bridge hanging over the river. That had to be the Saar, the Germany border.

The SS officers were enraged, and picked out fifty prisoners at random. Fortunately, I wasn't one of them, but I still had to watch. The guards threw about twenty-five spades at them and had them dig a deep trench, taking turns with the spades to hurry things up. Then the prisoners were lined up in front of it, and machine guns were moved into position. I watched the poor devils kiss their lives goodbye, certain that the bastards would go through with it and that who knew how many more of us would share the same fate afterwards.

I glanced at Leo and read his mind: we'd run as soon as the firing started. Suddenly, a soldier came running up to the officer in charge with a message for him. He stared at it, sighed with relief, and halted the execution.

The Germans unloaded enough armaments from that train to stop a Red Army offensive. Then they grouped us into marching order, the guards flanking us. Within an hour we had crossed the river over a narrow bridge and swung back again to the railroad tracks on the German side. A similar train of the same capacity was waiting for us. That was amazing logistics, considering the stage the war was at, with American and British fighter planes dominating the airspace and constantly seeking targets.

We were told that we were now in "civilized" Germany and would have to be more selective with our rest stops. They gave us some food and water and pushed us back into the cars. When the train started moving again, I began recognizing the names of the German stations as they passed.

Three more horrible days went by, with the train just creeping along, stopping repeatedly and sometimes switching tracks. Frankfurt . . . Fulda . . . Weimar . . . There was no question in my mind now: we were heading for Buchenwald.

Worst of all, after two desperate days looking for the slightest chance to escape, and knowing how not to miss a trick, and remembering how we'd succeeded in the past, Leo and I had to declare ourselves defeated.

We came to our last stop, the infamous Buchenwald camp. The station buzzed like a hive. Another train had just arrived, this one full of Polish prisoners. There were enough guards to handle all of us. We were prodded into line beside our cars, and a count was taken. Unlike other transports, which I had heard about from my German informants, every detainee had survived this one. Some of us weren't in good shape any more, but no one had died.

Then came the now infamous walk past the SS officers' barracks to the main gate with a huge factory in the distance.

"Arbeit Macht Frei" said the sign over the main entrance. *Work will set you free.* I asked myself: "Free from what?" I would learn the answer soon enough, inside those gates: "Free from life."

In despair, I turned to Leo.

"We didn't make it. Look where we've landed. The guard dogs, the towers, the SS pigs with their machine guns.

There's electric barbwire around the whole camp. How did we let this happen to us, just weeks before liberation?"

"Don't worry about it, Heinz," Leo answered calmly. "In the first place, we aren't dead yet. In the second place, if that's how it turns out, better men than us have already died in this war."

That was a good insight, not that it helped my mood. Even so, I forced myself to stay focused on his first point. He was right: we weren't dead yet, so let's keep up our spirits and do whatever we had to do.

The camp was packed with prisoners from all over the continent, speaking dozens of different languages. All were dressed in zebra uniforms, their heads shaved and their jackets marked. Most of them were wearing a red triangle with a letter above it. "F" for France, "P" for Poland, "R" for Russia, indicating that they were political prisoners. Only a few wore the green triangle of criminals, or the yellow six-point star of Jews, or the pink triangle of homosexuals (who were viewed as serious criminals by the Third Reich).

I found out quickly how some of these prisoners had survived for years in these camps, and what the armband they wore meant, the one that read "Kapo." That had exempted them from physical labor. It also kept them well fed and housed. In return, they did all the dirty work for their masters, keeping the other prisoners in line with so much brutal efficiency that the German guards were angels by comparison. It happened often that a prisoner couldn't control his hunger any more and stole a piece of bread from somebody. When caught doing that by a Kapo, he would be taken outside and literally beaten to death. The same treatment was reserved for other offences, such as being late for the twice-daily roll or slacking during a work detail. Once a Kapo took a dislike to you, your days were numbered. Sooner or later, he would find an excuse to eliminate you.

Buchenwald wasn't an extermination camp like Treblinka, but between the hunger, the hard labor, and the brutality, the death toll was high. When I arrived, the crematorium was going full blast, spewing out oily smoke and putrid vapor.

Our first order was to line up in front of a huge registration desk. The line was long. Prisoners from camps all over German-occupied Europe were arriving, having hastily been evacuated from territories now recaptured by the advancing Allies. It was a long time before I came within hearing of the registration desk, which was manned by SS officers aided by some interpreters.

Again, my mind was racing: Did they know what I'd been up to in France? Were they planning to finish the job their colleagues had started so well in Paris?

I focused my eyes and ears on the desk. The prisoners around me were all French, so I had the advantage of understanding the officers' questions in German before they were translated. To my amazement, I saw that the interrogators were working without any documents about us and were depending entirely on the answers supplied by the new arrivals, which they jotted down for their records.

Now it made sense to me. Our guards had retreated from Paris so quickly that they'd left our records behind. This was my chance. Over the next ten minutes, I worked feverishly to invent a new identity. Now came my turn.

"Name?"

"Heinz Martin."

"Nationality?"

"Dutch."

"Father?"

"Dutch."

"Mother?"

"German."

"What offence led to your arrest?"

Now the moment of truth—let's make it nice and easy.

"I was listening to the BBC in Paris when a neighbor walked in and turned me in to the authorities."

It was all written down. The officer seemed happy no to have to work with an interpreter and didn't ask any more questions.

Next we were all given zebra uniforms. They all looked alike to me and certainly weren't custom-tailored. By then my weight was down to about a hundred and thirty pounds, so I was able to find one that fit.

Before changing into our uniforms, we had to shower and get deloused. By that point, the gas chambers at Auschwitz and other camps were common knowledge. But fortunately for all of us, the showers at Buchenwald were real. They deloused us by spraying us with a powder.

Next came the "beauty parlor." Dozens of chairs were lined up with some, well-fed, well-groomed prisoners behind them, equipped with clippers. In next to no time, I was bald. Now I was officially a member of Buchenwald society.

The first few days passed in idleness. We received our meager meals—a watery soup and the occasional piece of horrible-tasting brown bread. The camp was so packed with newcomers that there were no bunks for us in the barracks. We had to spend the first week outside, covered only in a blanket. Fortunately, the weather held. As it turned out, we'd see much worse.

When I was finally assigned to a barrack, the smell was unbearable. Also, the prisoners were constantly fighting over stolen blankets and bread. Worst of all, the fleas were eating me alive. Never before had I seen them that size, and never again. The fleas of Buchenwald were so big you could feel them land on your body.

Prisoners kept arriving daily. Most of them were being shipped from the east, one step ahead of the Red Army. They'd already survived years of hunger and torture. They were rough men, and they didn't feel the hardship as much as the city-bred prisoners from the west. I met one group that had survived this long for another reason: they were musicians. The Nazis had formed them into an orchestra and had supplied them with instruments. They played beautiful music, and some of them were singers. Their morale was unusually high. Somehow everyone must have liked them, since most of them had lived through Auschwitz so far and had been sent west just before its liberation by the Red Army.

A few German political prisoners had survived, mainly socialists and communists. By now they had lost their political fire, and plenty of them had been assigned soft tasks like distributing food or running the laundry or drawing up daily work schedules. Jobs like that meant adequate food and a chance to feather one's nest.

The political prisoners were good people to know, and our common language allowed me to develop a good relationship with one of them, a guy named Martin. He was a socialist and had been arrested shortly after Hitler took power in 1933. It astonished me that he'd survived eleven gruesome years. The stories he told me were fascinating. He used to tell me about some of the sadistic acts he'd witnessed on the part of the guards. One of them—

The camp commander's wife, quite young in those days, had her own idea of fun with the prisoners. One day before the war, when the inmates weren't undernourished yet, she appeared on the site of a work commando while they were digging a trench. In a loud, provoking voice, she addressed the men, lifting up her skirt to flash her genitals. The trench was narrow, which made it possible for her to walk broad-legged over it. The men were digging in it bent over.

"Everybody notice that I'm not wearing any panties?"

With that, she drew her gun from its holster, cocked it, and announced, "I'm going to walk slowly over the trench while you guys are digging. If one of you bastards stops work or even looks up, you're dead." Then she made her slow death walk over the heads of desperate young men, who hadn't had a woman for an eternity, teasing them and goading them to look up and touch her.

The weather turned cooler, and life in Buchenwald got worse. Days and weeks passed, food was getting extremely scarce, and the Allies were nowhere in sight. What was different was the sky. We could hear squadrons of British and American bombers flying overhead day and night. The flak guns were still active, but there were no German fighter planes to be seen.

One morning I heard the familiar roar of the B-17s in the distance. I expected them to fly on to Berlin or to one of the German industrial cities. Instead, moments later, I saw a lead plane overhead, marking the sky with smoke. Now the air-alert sirens started sounding. A squadron of bombers followed shortly, and all hell broke loose. Every plane unloaded its cargo as it reached the smoke signal. I hit the ground, flat on my stomach, alongside one of the barracks, and felt the detonations shake the ground under me.

After a few minutes, we heard the all-clear signal. I got up and saw smoke drifting up from the camp. But most of it was rising from just outside the barbwire. There was a serious fire in the Gusdorf Works, the nearby factory where Buchenwald prisoners worked shifts.

Within a few days, the eyewitness reports began trickling in: all the SS officers' homes outside the camp had been flattened, the factory had been almost completely flattened, though fortunately, few prisoners had died. Only one bomb had missed its target, hitting the laundry building inside the camp. Miraculously, there hadn't been any casualties. Pretty good shooting by Uncle Sam.

That turned out to be my last memorable experience in Buchenwald's main camp. I had heard already that there were smaller work camps near high-priority war industries in the heart of Germany. Some privileged inmates, like the politicals, were going to be transferred to those factories, where a decent amount of food would be supplied them. There was a disadvantage, of course: the Allied bombers would be targeting those same places.

My luck held out: I was one of the few lucky ones to be sent to a camp in the suburbs of Leipzig.

13

THE LIBERATION

OUR DEPARTURE FROM Buchenwald was more dignified than our arrival. A bus was waiting for us at the gate. Though we stood out because of our shaved heads and zebra uniforms, and were heavily guarded by SS men, we could already sense the reduced discipline. They needed us, and we knew it.

Through the bus window, I saw that the houses with their little front yards that lined the road leading out of the camp had been reduced to rubble. Our bus started moving, this time filled only to normal capacity. The hundred-mile ride to Leipzig was a pleasant break from camp life. The people in the towns we passed minded their own business, heads down to their daily chores. Halfway to Leipzig, we passed a military airport. I couldn't believe my eyes—the entire field and all the runways were packed with Messerschmitt fighters, yet during the massive American air raid a week before there hadn't been a single German plane in the sky.

The guard next to me was staring at the field as well, and must have read my mind. "Kein Sprit," he muttered. No gasoline. No wonder the Allies had ruled the sky for months.

A little later we saw Leipzig in the distance. As we drew closer, I saw that it had been almost flattened by the recent air raids. Our bus drove through a gate and stopped in front of a cluster of barracks surrounded by barbwire on the factory grounds. A reserved-looking man in military uniform supplied us with blankets and assigned our bunks to us. Then we were fed some soup, which was definitely thicker than at Buchenwald, and received a small portion of bread, which tasted just as awful as before.

Next morning early, we were marched into a spruce-looking building that the bombers hadn't found yet. We were asked to sit down in a classroom with a huge blackboard at the front, just as if we were human beings. The instructor, flanked by a French interpreter, began drawing something that looked like an engine cylinder.

He addressed the class in German.

"You people in this room are privileged to participate in our war effort. We will give you a short training period here and then will transfer you to a nearby factory four hundred metres underground, where we are manufacturing vital parts. Precision is vital, and I am here to teach you just that."

The interpreter repeated the introduction in French. Then the instructor wrote the drawing's measurements on the blackboard.

"This is one of the items you will be producing on the lathe. Let's make sure you know how to measure."

This was too good to be true. I knew the answers already before they were even asked in French, and made quite an impression on the instructor.

At the end of the first class, he walked over to me and asked, "Are you able to communicate with these people and tell them in French what you learned today?"

"Of course," I answered quickly.

"Then I want you to walk with me tomorrow to all the operators of the different machines I will assign to them and make my instructions clear."

The next day we were brought into a large machine shop. Two people were placed on each lathe, and the instructor went from machine to machine with a piece of material and demonstrated to his students how to operate the controls. I was eager to learn the procedure, since I was being bombarded with questions from my fellow prisoners and had to translate them for the instructor. He was professional and humane in his responses, which almost made me forget that I'd been treated like the scum of the earth only a week ago.

We kept returning to the classroom for one hour each day and were ready to move to the actual plant after two weeks. A bus brought us to the village of Wansleben, to what had been a salt mine. The property was surrounded by barbwire, with two guard towers. The barracks held about two thousand prisoners of different nationalities. Among them were three other inmates who were marked with the same initial I was wearing, "N" for Netherlands. I avoided them as much as I could, since I wasn't keen on answering their questions about what was supposed to be our common country.

The other prisoners soon told me that the workers had to descend every morning early by elevator thirteen hundred feet into a mine, where shops had been set up to manufacture parts for the VI and V2 rockets. The average working day was fourteen hours, seven days a week. It seemed that those godforsaken rockets were my destiny for this war.

The accommodations in this camp were double bunk beds in very large rooms on various levels of a converted factory. There was a roll call shortly after we arrived in the yard. I was reminded that the SS was still well and alive here.

The commandant strutted in front of us and told us there would be no tolerance for breaking camp rules or falling behind on any work assignment. He was flanked by two cruel-looking prisoners wearing "Kapo" armbands and the letter "P" (Poland) on their jackets. I had no doubt they were eager to carry out any orders given by him. Then he strode through our lines, walked up close to some inmates he chose at random, and lifted their heads high up with a club he was carrying.

"You want to be a good boy and work very hard down in the mine, don't you?"

I noticed that anyone who answered too quietly or too loudly received a blow from his club. It happened with answers in either direction. Now I knew for sure this wasn't the place to stand out. Just mind your own business and report your number when questioned. 72138, clearly marked on my jacket.

After a long roll call, which had us standing for two hours in the same spot in the nasty East German winter, he gave us a chance to stretch our legs.

Once inside, I received my bunk assignment. I could not have been luckier with the neighbors I found. They would turn out to be true friends and the reason I survived the last five months of the war.

When I approached the fourplex of bunks, two upper and two lower ones, their occupants were on them already, except for one lower one, which was mine. I glanced at my bunkmates and saw that they were all wearing the initial "R."

So I was bunking with Russians. That wasn't necessarily good news, because the Soviet Union still had a high illiteracy rate, which could make for very dull company. I was in for a surprise. Their spokesman reached out his hand to me and said in perfect German, "My name is Lev, and these are my two comrades, Alexis and Peter. I'm from Moscow and my friends come from Leningrad. What is your name, and what is your hometown?"

We shook hands and I introduced myself. That first night I was only able to learn their professions. They were deeply reserved and sophisticated, yet somehow they also radiated warmth.

Lev, the ultimate intellectual, was a chemical engineer by profession. Alexis, much taller and stronger, had more trouble with the German language and also worked as a chemical engineer back home. Peter, the youngest and the most reserved, a sweet, clean-cut boy, had been attending university when he was swept into the war.

Next morning early, we received some of that horrible bread and attended our roll call in front of the elevator. Fortunately, it didn't take long, and we proceeded into the shaft. After descending for what seemed like eternity, the mine cage stopped and we disembarked for the long walk to our workshop. Prisoners who had finished the night shift were passing us in the opposite direction, looking exhausted.

The smell of salt was overwhelming as we entered a large, noisy cavern filled with the machinery we were going to operate. A few German technicians were expecting us. They guided us to our assigned lathes and gave us instructions. They were professional and courteous about it.

For the first few hours, I worked like everyone else and even found it interesting to be exposed to a new work experience. Fortunately, this sort of mass production work never bored me. During lunch break, while I was spooning down the watery soup, one of the German foremen approached me.

"Are you the guy who speaks German?"

"Yes, sir," I answered with relief.

"I want you to be available to me at all times," he said. "Especially during the first few weeks, when I still have a lot of instructions for your friends for them to do the job correctly."

He pointed at a table with a pile of blueprints and a few chairs.

"This will be your station. Familiarize yourself with the plans so that I can call on you whenever I need you."

This could be a fantastic break for me. The less physical work I had to perform, the longer I could stay alive on these food rations.

The German technician turned out to be a nonpolitical man, completely devoted to his work and quite friendly toward me. He provided me with a daily newspaper, censored of course, but I had learned to read between the lines and became the official supplier of war news in the camp. He even tossed me a piece of bread here and there and made sure I had enough to do at my station that I never had to go back to the lathe again.

Another pleasant experience awaited me upstairs. My three Russian sleeping companions and I got involved in long conversations. Lev told me that all three of them had been officers before being captured and interned in a prisoner-of-war camp.

"How did you end up in a concentration camp?" I asked.

"It's an unusual story," he told me. "Our belief in true Communism is strong, so we didn't stop preaching to our less educated comrades during our internment. The camp commander got wind of it and decided we were dangerous conspirators. He labeled us political and no longer to be protected by the Geneva Convention. So we wound up in Buchenwald. Fortunately, because of our professions, we're here now."

These three men conducted themselves as living examples of the Communist Manifesto. There was never any pushing for food or special treatment. Any rations they received were consolidated and then split into exactly three. It was a delight to watch them.

I was closest to Lev. Many times we spent half the night thinking about our lives after the war, knowing that we most likely would go in entirely opposite directions.

Otherwise, life in the factory was monotonous. I got hold of a French–German dictionary and was able to improve my French by studying during working hours. My German foreman welcomed it and backed me up in this activity.

One day, I got up feeling dreadful. My temperature must have been way up. I forced myself down into the mine, my head hammering, barely able to stand. Hoping to persuade the orderly to send me back to my sack again, I was trying to kill time at my station. When he finally came around, I reported my condition to him.

"Sorry to hear it," he answered. "We don't know any sick people in this place. There are only two categories—healthy ones or dead ones. Which will it be?"

Then he handed me a pill with the words, "Back to work."

My daily newspapers kept me well informed. Just judging by the German High Command's own words, I knew that the day of our liberation couldn't be far. By now my foreman was treating me as an equal.

March 1945 came around. It was time to prepare a final escape. The most important thing would be to cover up my bald head, since it would be an immediate giveaway among the Germans. Also, my zebra outfit would have to disappear the moment I hit the road. I asked my German superior, who entered and left the camp daily, to supply me with some headgear and a set of long underwear.

He looked at me with a puzzled smile.

"Now, when spring is around the corner, you want warmer clothes?"

Then he turned away with an understanding gesture.

A week later, he handed me a package containing a dark-blue sport cap and a set of long winter underwear. That suited me fine. I was confident that I could walk around in this outfit for a few hours at least.

April 11, 1945, was a warm, pleasant spring day. Our shift in the mine was abruptly called off at midday. We ascended in the elevators immediately and met our nervous guards at the top.

"Everyone to his bunk at once."

After about an hour, there was a roll call. All the prisoners were assembled except for the ones in the infirmary. The SS commander addressed us with a grim look on his face.

"The American General Patton is penetrating our Fatherland with his heavy tanks. We are in direct line of his dangerous sandwich movement. Within a few days our Führer will deliver the final blow to them, as soon as our miracle weapon is ready to be launched. Until then, we have to move east as quickly as we can. We don't have any vehicles available, so our march will be on foot. You will receive all the food we now have in our storage rooms so that you can strengthen yourself for this march. Don't get any ideas—I have brought in reinforcement guards who will flank you on both sides. The slightest attempt at escape will be punished immediately by death. My men have strict instructions to carry out my orders."

I looked around and saw indeed a tremendous increase in guards, all armed with rifles. A closer look, though, gave me comfort. They were all regular Wehrmacht, and most of them not so young anymore.

Back at our bunks, we received soup with some meat in it this time, and plenty of bread. I saw that most of the prisoners were stuffing it in, not realizing that their empty stomachs wouldn't take it so well. Many of them got so sick that the march, once it started, would be unendurable for them.

My Russian friends cautioned me not to eat too much, and my own intuition gave me confidence that I'd soon be free again.

We left the camp around five p.m., all two thousand of us, in a long column, four abreast. Guards flanked us, some of them SS but most of them Wehrmacht. I managed to position myself on the outside right. The nearest guard, who walked at times ahead of me and at times behind me, was a war-weary soldier in his early forties.

It wasn't long before we struck up a conversation. After I learned how much he wanted to get this damned war over with and return home to his family, I concentrated just on that subject. He seemed relieved at the chance to talk freely about his family life to someone who seemed to understand. He smiled at me whenever he passed me.

It was still daylight, and the Germans we passed were staring at us with hate. Something told me I had better escape the first chance I got.

Dusk was setting in, and I noticed some light flashes accompanied by detonations on the western horizon. That had to be the front and would be my destination.

After dark we entered a village. The narrow streets were deserted. We must have been marching for four hours. I wanted to make my move *now*.

I looked around and saw my "friend" walking ahead of me and no guard visible behind me. We were almost in the center of the village, and I was almost brushing the walls with my right shoulder. Then came a wide-open door to a barn. Without hesitating, I leaned my body into it, stepped through, and closed it softly. Then I froze in place, not daring to breathe.

Ten or fifteen minutes passed. I could get it from either side yet. An ambitious SS guard could pick me out with a flashlight, or the farmer could surprise me and turn me in. I understood the gamble I'd just taken—an early escape from this transport column would be treated as a precedent.

By now the entire column had moved on, and I was still wearing my zebra uniform. I had to proceed with extreme caution and get out of this village immediately. I crawled on my stomach across the road, between two houses, and into the open field. Then I walked briskly in the direction of the dawn.

Once I considered myself far enough from the village, I stopped. I pulled my cap out of my pocket and placed it on my shaved head. Then I took my stripes off, buried them under a bush, and kept walking in my long underwear straight across the fields.

I was definitely moving in the right direction, because the lightning and explosions grew more severe. Then suddenly the earth began to tremble and I could hear the sound of heavy chains.

Spring was in the air. I felt comfortable in my heavy underwear. The chirping of birds was the first sound I remember of my newly obtained freedom. I was ready to embrace the whole world, but I knew I hadn't made it quite yet.

Stay cool, I told myself, don't screw up now of all times. You've been on your feet for twenty hours. Don't do anything irrational. Rest now so that you can assess your situation when daylight comes.

That was my inner voice, and I listened to it.

There wasn't any sign of civilization around me, so I planted myself beside a bush and closed my eyes. Oh, this sweet feeling of freedom. Was I dreaming, or had I really survived this terrible war? Nothing would matter after this. If I lived through this, I'd live through anything.

Feeling strong yet humble, I dozed off.

A loud explosion made me jump to my feet. I saw smoke in the distance and the sun on the horizon.

I began walking stealthily toward the front line, ears cocked for more explosions. After another hour walking through fields, I came to a highway and turned west.

Soon after, I ran into a group of German soldiers, seemingly coming from the front and dragging their bodies in apathy. Some of them were bandaged, and no one even glanced as I passed them going the other way. Their sergeant was trailing them, and he, too, had passed me already.

Then he suddenly changed his mind and turned around.

"Du, halte!"

This was the moment of truth. We had to be less than a few miles from the front, and the strongest of us was going to prevail here without any questions asked. Most likely he'd been fighting for years and was used to blindly taking and dishing out orders. But what must he be thinking now?

Of course . . . From my strange-looking outfit that close to the front line, he must think I'm a deserter. That was something for me to work with. I'd give him the most opposite impression of a soldier he'd ever seen. He'd never think I was one.

I turned around and answered slowly and annoyed.

"Was ist los?"

"Why you are walking right into the firing line, while everyone else is trying to escape from there?"

175

"Mister"—this was addressing a German officer—"I'm a Dutchman and was bombed out yesterday at the Nordhausen factory during the big raid." (I'd received that much information last night from my German "friend.") "Look at me, these are all the clothes I've got left. My family's in Holland so that's where I'm walking. I've had it, I'm going home."

His eyes bored through me while I stood there calmly. After an eternity, he let me continue.

That was a close one. I didn't know any more which danger was greater—the Germans on this side of the front or the American artillery ahead of me.

I decided to take my chances with the latter, since the Allies weren't aiming at me specifically, and kept walking west on the road. Some German military vehicles went flying past from the front at breakneck speed. They knew that the Allied planes were dominating the sky, ready to descend on anything that moved.

Now I entered the real battle zone, with shells landing all around me. Just then an unexpected opportunity entered my life. When I turned the next corner, I saw a large farmhouse with an old woman standing at the entrance. She was bawling her eyes out, looking around helplessly.

I rushed over and asked her in German if I could help her.

She was hysterical and had a hard time talking to me. Then the words finally came out.

"I survived the war so far, never been hungry, I've been able to feed my family, I had a letter from my son last week, and he's still alive. Now we're about to be overrun by American tanks. They'll destroy our property and kill us all."

I put my arm around her, trying to gain her confidence, and spoke to her firmly.

"Little mother, listen close to me. Do what I say and you and your family won't get a scratch. Let's go inside, into the cellar so we don't get hit by a shell. Then take the biggest white bedsheet you have and hang it out a window facing the front. The Americans aren't savages. They won't harm you if you make it clear to them you won't resist."

"But our Wehrmacht will punish us when they see the white flag."

"The Wehrmacht is too busy running from the Americans," I told her. "They have their own problems and couldn't care less what you do."

She saw I meant it. Within minutes, we'd converted her farmhouse into a bomb shelter. The foundation was strong, and we felt very secure there, expecting any moment an American officer to show his face and check us out.

Instead, the rumbling of the Shermans remained in the distance. Meanwhile, ten or so more people entered our shelter over the next hour. They came from all walks of life. Women and children, an elderly soldier, a French worker, all of them hoping to save their skin. I asked every newcomer what was doing out there and always got the same answer: the Americans were turning north at the crossroads two miles away.

I had lost my patience and went looking for myself. Once on the road, I saw that we were in no man's land now and that the fighting had taken a ninety-degree turn. Anxious to reach the American lines, I started a brisk walk, along the way meeting up with some other slave laborers who were eager to see their homes again.

The trembling of the earth grew more intense, and then the road turned toward an intersection. A gigantic Sherman tank was blocking it, its turret gun pointed straight at us. In the near distance beyond it we saw troops and more tanks heading north. A soldier in a uniform I had only seen in movies was sitting on the turret looking us over carefully. He was wearing the number 7 on his sleeve.

As soon as I thought he could hear me, I dug up my best school English, lifted my cap, and shouted, "I am a friend and arrive from concentration camp."

He stared at my shaved head for a moment, then laughed and threw me a pack of cigarettes.

My walking companions of the last two miles stared at me in amazement, since I hadn't told them my true identity. A few soldiers walked up to us, checked us for weapons, and asked us a few questions about our past and our destination.

They released me after a few minutes. Now I was free to continue on to the newly occupied American zone. I'd promised to report to the 7th Army headquarters in Eisleben.

The horrors of the war became very distinct now. The bodies of German soldiers and the skeletons of destroyed tanks and vehicles lined the road. Now that the battle was over here, and before a new military government was in place, slave workers and the local Germans were looting the stores.

I walked through the chaos, minding my own business. American heavy armor kept rolling in the opposite direction, and I yearned to join the action somehow. Finally, late in the afternoon, I reached Eisleben, where enough signs had been posted that I found the military HQ without a problem.

The desk sergeant looked hard at me when I walked in. I found out later that I was the first escaped political prisoner in the area.

"I just escaped from concentration camp Buchenwald," I told him. "I need food and housing and also want to offer my services."

He looked helplessly at me and finally answered: "Just wait here. I think this is a case for the lieutenant."

Moments later, he returned and showed me to another office.

"Captain Spiegel, C.I.C.," read the nameplate on his desk. A dark-haired officer and I studied each other. It must have been love at first sight. I felt myself relax just at the sight of him. I told him my story in as few words as I could. He believed me, and gave me a big welcome.

"Okay, Heinz, after what you went through, I'll put you up in the best hotel in town with an excellent kitchen. Check in and relax for a few days and fill your stomach slowly. Then come back to my office and report to me. I think I have some interesting work for you."

On my way out, I saw the Armed Forces newspaper, *Stars and Stripes,* on the desk. The large headline announced:

PRESIDENT ROOSEVELT IS DEAD.

14
POST-WAR REACTIONS

I TOOK A PLEASANT room with a big bed and white sheets—an almost forgotten luxury. Then I went down to the dining room and enjoyed my first full meal in freedom. I was tired enough to hit the sack soon after, and must have slept into the middle of the next day. After a midday meal, I strolled through the ancient town of Eisleben, where Martin Luther was born.

The Americans had taken over the district, but no one had bothered yet to take down the Nazi propaganda posters. Swastikas were still all over town and in many windows. Something had to be done about that.

For a few days, I took it nice and easy. I was allowed to buy some clothes in one of the stores and started feeling like a human again. My natural disposition came back to me. There were feelings of hatred toward the guilty ones who were responsible for all the crimes committed against my family, my friends, and me. But I also felt love for others, and I yearned for companionship.

I solved the latter problem quickly. I met a nice German girl who had been orphaned by the war and was very understanding of my situation. I spent most of my non-working hours with her, and it was interesting to compare notes, since we'd been on opposite sides for the past few years.

Lieutenant Spiegel was waiting for me when I showed up a few days later.

"So, Heinz, are you rested and ready for action?"

"Willing and eager. Just assign me to missions you're having a hard time handling. I know the German mentality."

"Okay. Let's start this afternoon. You'll accompany my sergeant and a few men to a nearby village. We know that three of our flyers were shot down there, and I want to make sure they had a decent burial, which I doubt. I want you to be the liaison between the Germans and ourselves."

I rode in a small truck with a sergeant from Brooklyn and three more soldiers in the back. I hit it off with the sergeant immediately. When we got to the village, we looked for the mayor, who pointed to where the airmen had been buried.

After we inspected the site, the sergeant decided they should be reburied in the village cemetery in individual graves with their own identification.

"That's gonna be quite a job for us, Heinz. We sure could use help."

"Help you will have," I answered. "Just give me the ignition key and I'll return soon."

It was a pleasure to drive a powerful American vehicle, and I returned to the mayor.

"I want you to assign five able-bodied men immediately to do some digging, and by the way, you'll be the sixth."

The mayor looked aghast that he would have to do work beneath his dignity, but I didn't give him much time to think about it. "Come on," I insisted. "Let's get moving.

The job has to be finished before dusk, and the sergeant is waiting."

That he understood, and quickly rounded up five big, obedient guys. I packed them into the vehicle and delivered them to the burial site.

My sergeant, who had already started the job, gave me a big welcome and a pat on the shoulder.

"You even recruited the mayor? I would have never had the nerve."

"Just stick around, Joe, you'll learn."

The mission went flawlessly and efficiently. Three American airmen had a decent burial before darkness set in, and we had a very happy lieutenant on our hands.

The next day's assignment was a little more exciting. We'd been told that an SS officer was in hiding somewhere nearby. We had to find and arrest him and get as much information out of him as possible.

My American friends were armed to the teeth, submachine guns and all. According to CIC rules, I wasn't allowed to carry a weapon. We started out, and I looked at my sergeant.

"Joe, you guys are carrying a whole arsenal, and I feel naked without anything but my bare hands."

"Okay, but don't tell the lieutenant I let you carry my handgun during this mission."

"Thank you, it's better than nothing. At least I know how to handle it—and don't stop me if I do, if that bastard gets any ideas."

We found a man in civilian clothes in a small apartment in the village. Joe approached him with the direct message: "We have information that you're SS Sturmführer Otte."

I watched his expression. The surprise lasted for less than a second, then he answered with arrogance: "There must be a mistake, my name is Horst Muller. Here is my identification. I was a corporal in the army."

He was well covered by our men, but knowing what violence the SS was capable of, I jumped forward when he reached into his pocket.

"Freeze and turn around."

To me, he had SS written all over him—in his look, in his mannerisms. We searched him thoroughly for weapons. He was clean.

"Joe," I said, "let me have him for a few minutes." He nodded yes.

Gestapo headquarters in Paris was still vivid in my mind, and I knew the only language they understood. I walked up close to him and in a gentle voice in his mother tongue, asked: "Do you know me?"

185

"No, I've never seen you before."

With that, I took another step toward him and punched him in the mouth with all my strength. He was bleeding slightly, and looked at me in astonishment.

"Now that we've got to know each other, take off your jacket and your shirt."

He seemed unsettled by that request, but didn't have any choice while staring down the barrel of a gun. I lifted his left arm and pointed to a tattoo under his armpit, a sure sign of the SS.

"Case closed, Herr Sturmführer, you're under arrest."

When we brought him back to headquarters. Captain Spiegel had a lot of questions to ask. He was still uncooperative and forced me at times to apply his own method of interrogation. It certainly relieved me of a lot of frustration, and the CIC gained from it.

I was about to leave the office when I saw two camp survivors at the reception desk. The attendant called me over for help establishing their genuineness. They looked at me, and we embraced immediately. My Russian friends Lev and Alexis had made it. I turned to the attendant.

"They're more than clean—they're friends of mine, and I'd be very thankful if you put them up at the same hotel."

My request was granted, and after completing the necessary paperwork, we all walked to the hotel.

While they filled their stomachs, they began to unburden themselves about the past week. I was eager to hear about the fate of my co-prisoners after my escape.

"We marched for five days and five nights with very little rest, until finally the Americans caught up and surrounded us. Five hundred of us—that's one-quarter—didn't make it. When they were too weak to continue, they were shot in the neck. Our guards tried to tell the American officers that they were only doing their duty and following orders. Most of them bought the story, but a few of us survivors who still had the strength to speak were able to convince the commanding officer there were big differences in the behavior of our guards. Some of them killed like the sadists they were, others were more lenient. He finally asked us to divide them into three groups: The good guys, the medium ones, and the killers. They were taken away in different trucks according to our classifications. Our comrades were set free and distributed in different towns. Peter wound up in another place, and here we are, ready to celebrate our liberation with you."

"Quite a story, Lev. I'm glad I got away early. Listen, I got to know an American MP. I think he can get us some booze and might even want to join us in our celebration."

"Sounds good, Heinz, let's do it."

Benjamin Klein, from Passaic, New Jersey, and his partner were the most visible military policemen in Eisleben. They had the task of enforcing the curfew for German civilians and making sure the soldiers of the 7th Army behaved themselves. Our hotel was on the town's main square, and Ben sometimes hung out with us once he was sure the village was under control. We chatted a lot and exchanged stories about our recent lives, as well as dreams of the future.

I heard about the garment center of New York, where he worked, and his one-hour commute across the Hudson River to suburbia, where he lived with his folks. He was the proud owner of an Oldsmobile; he could afford to buy all the good food he liked in the well-stocked supermarkets; he could even go out dancing on Saturdays or drive to the beach in the summertime, all on his salary.

I was acquiring the first taste of that country of unlimited opportunities, and my desire grew to make a new life there. Ben liked the idea of celebrating our liberation and promised to find the needed liquid by the following night.

Lev, Alexis, and I had a job to do before the party. Both of them were still badly shaken by having to witness the executions of their comrades. So together we pledged to clean the town of Eisleben of all swastikas, and to do it in one day. Most of the time, Alexis's tough demeanor and perfect German was enough to convince people.

"The war is over for you," he'd tell the ones who hesitated. "Hitler isn't your Führer any more, and we don't want to be reminded of him. Take it down by order of the American military government."

Captain Spiegel only smiled when he heard about it.

As you might expect, the Germans were pointing fingers by then and acting out of jealousy of their neighbors. That led me to an important piece of information, which I kept to myself until the right time came to use it.

A high-ranking Nazi, who didn't have a military record and wasn't on the local wanted list, had returned from Berlin to his home village nearby. So far he was enjoying his freedom, and all the food from his farm. He even had a beautiful white car hidden in his barn. That, indeed, was interesting. I managed to learn his name and party record, then got directions to his farm.

Just after dinner, Ben showed his face with another MP and told us, "I brought you something special tonight, you guys from Eastern Europe will appreciate it." Turning to Lev and Alexis, he said: "A bottle of Slibowitz."

Little did I realize how effective plum brandy can be. My Russian friends brought out water glasses for everyone and started making toasts. Ben and his partner, who were off that night, knew better and took only small sips. Alexis challenged me and lifted his glass.

"Let's see how good you are, Heinz. This is how we drink in Russia, and you wouldn't insult me. Bottoms up."

He wasn't waiting for anyone and turned his words into deeds. Lev followed his example, and both of them looked happy and normal. Their eyes rested on me with a clear message: *Come on, you coward.*

I was shamed into it, so I did it. The room began to spin, my vision went blurry. That's the last thing I remember. Ben told me the next day that they had to carry me to my room, undress me, and tuck me into bed.

Lev and Alexis had been liberated in their zebra uniforms. We borrowed a third from an ex-prisoner—they were drifting a few at a time into Eisleben by now. I slipped into it one last time, and the three of us went to a photographer to have our picture taken as a souvenir of all the months we'd starved together behind barbwire. They also took me to a victory celebration in a schoolyard, where Stalin delivered an enthusiastic speech through the loudspeakers. The highlight was the announcement that the American 1st Army and the Red Army had just linked up on the Elbe at Torgau.

The next day, *Stars and Stripes* printed photographs of Russians and American soldiers dancing, drinking, and hugging each other.

The war in Europe was wrapping up quickly. Within a few days, Hitler had committed suicide and Berlin had fallen to the Red Army. Finally, on May 8, we all celebrated V-E Day.

There was a big parade of all Allied forces in and around Eisleben. The ex-prisoners and "enemies" of the

Reich were delirious with joy, and booze flowed like water. The American combat troops had been replaced by the occupation forces. I was transferred to the new German police and worked with them for a couple of weeks. Then I got restless: suddenly I couldn't wait to return to Essen in the hope of finding some of my family.

One evening, after I left the police station, I made my move. I asked a coworker, who had also gone through the mill in the war, to ride along with me. We found the farmhouse easily, and since it was after curfew, my target had to be home.

We flashed our IDs as soon as we entered and strutted our authority right from the start.

"We have information about your activities in Berlin," I started out. "The American commander is very interested and has ordered us to interrogate you. Remember, telling us the truth can only benefit you, because we will find out anyway and will not reward you for your lies."

My plan was to drag out the investigation and tire him out. At the same time, I would have to give him enough rope to hang himself, since my knowledge about his past was limited. But he was cooperative, perhaps because his activities in the war wouldn't make him a priority for any war crimes prosecution.

I judged that the occupation forces wouldn't be too interested in him just then—there were much bigger catches to be made. Even so, he was a high-ranking Nazi, so

I decided, for vengeance and for my own benefit, to make my next move.

"Your case sounds serious, and I'll supply the commander with the information I gathered from you tonight. He'll decide whether you can remain free or not."

I got up, looked him in the eye, and continued:

"Meanwhile, we have a security problem with you. We know you have hidden an automobile in your barn, and that we cannot tolerate."

He turned pale and was breathing heavily. I made one more step toward him, reaching out with my open right hand:

"The ignition key, and the papers!"

He was upset, but he followed my order. We flanked him while he walked over to a desk and opened a drawer. After digging around for a moment, he produced both items. I took them from him, explaining: "You understand that in your position you cannot register this vehicle. Furthermore, our office is in dire need of transportation to clean up the mess in this country that people like you created. So, let's go to the barn and get this automobile moving."

He looked as if he had just died a thousand deaths, but he also knew that an order was an order. He led us to another building on his property and swung open the door. After we removed a layer of hay, we saw the front grill of a beautiful white Adler Trumpf Junior.

My heart beat faster at the thought that I would be one of the privileged few that year to drive a car in Germany—especially one in mint condition.

He removed some more hay and blankets to uncover it completely. There it was, a white beauty with good tires and immaculate upholstery. The tires were especially important, because no one anywhere had rubber at that time; you couldn't even get it on the black market. He got in the car with us and gave us a few pointers.

Then he turned the key and started the engine. Right from the start it ran beautifully, as if the engine had just been tuned. The fuel gauge showed some gasoline left, and that was important, too. Gas in those days was available only for official business or to those with plenty of clout.

"Good night, old man," I said. "We'll borrow this for a while and get back to you to continue our investigation. Don't make a move—you're already marked."

I drove away with my object of self-bestowed restitution. My friend followed me in the other car.

15

REUNION

TIME WAS PRESSING. I wasn't going to wait around to learn the repercussions of what I'd just done, or to confront a superior who might question my actions or even want this beautiful car to himself. I drove to my hotel, packed, and drove west. Destination: Essen an der Ruhr.

Fortunately, I found a good road map in the glove compartment. It told me I had about 350 kilometers ahead of me. The roads were in poor condition because of all the heavy equipment and tanks that had moved over them recently, in both directions. Also, I wasn't a very experienced driver at the time. The biggest problem, though, was finding enough gas.

I decided to drive another hour or two that night, which would get me almost to Göttingen. I might be able to fill up there, if I tried early enough in the morning, in which case I could be in Essen by nightfall.

Petrol was strictly rationed and only available with coupons. I had learned the procedure through my work with the police. After a few hours' sleep on the roadside, I drove into town, looked for the municipal building, and found the Bureau of Motor Vehicles.

It negotiated with the superintendent for 20 liters worth of coupons. First I had to convince him, with the help of my credentials and some persuasive talk, that I was on a vital mission. Finally I succeeded. Now I could make it to my destination with one more fill-up.

The rest of the trip was both pleasant and frustrating. I enjoyed driving, but I also had to contend with the mangled roads and the rubble of bombed-out towns and bridges.

The full extent of the destruction appeared before me now. Though I'd been glad of the chance to help defeat Nazi Germany, I felt for the people who had survived this long. Now I watched them scavenging for food and using anything with wheels to move their belongings. They were pushing their handcarts down the road and peddling their bicycles, busily transporting materials to turn their destroyed homes into temporary shelters. I reminded myself that they couldn't all have been war criminals.

True enough, only a few of them had dared speak against their government, and fewer still resisted it directly. That made most of them guilty, but show me that the people in other countries, in the same circumstances, wouldn't have done the same. The stories about noble Resistance fighters in the German-occupied countries are endless, but their battle was against an intruder, not a self-proclaimed savior of a nation at a time of economic disaster.

I would have to seek out the resisters and listen to the rest with an open mind. I began wondering whether I should help the well-meaning Germans rise from the ashes and rebuild their country under a democracy.

Late in the evening I arrived in the western suburbs of Essen, or what was left of it. I didn't recognize the neighborhood where my sister and her family had been living when I fled to Holland. It was after curfew, the streets were deserted. I knocked on several doors to ask directions—no way would I find the house otherwise. The destruction was overwhelming.

Finally, I found an apartment building that I remembered vaguely as being the address of my sister's friends. Hannes Van Dooren opened the door and gave me a look of annoyed suspicion.

"I'm Heinz," I told him. "Irma's brother."

Hannes stared at me, then gave me a big bear hug with his powerful arms: "You survived!" he shouted. "That's wonderful! Come in, Martha will fix you some dinner if you'll settle for what little we have. You'll also spend the night with us."

"Where are Irma and Julius?" I asked.

"Don't worry, Heinz, they're safe in a small town in Westphalia, not too far from here."

I entered the apartment and got a big welcome from his wife. We hadn't known each other before the war, but we were all wound up enough to chatter into the middle of the night. The next morning, Hannes offered to accompany me to Billerbeck, a picturesque town near Münster.

It was Sunday, and we arrived about mid-morning in the center of town. Hannes knew we would have to get some local directions to find the farmhouse where Irma was living. Moving automobiles were rare in those days, and anybody driving one would have to know the area well.

We parked on the market square and stopped a car that was approaching slowly.

"Sorry to bother you, but would you know by any chance where Julius and Irma Spitmann live?"

The driver looked at me with curiosity and asked, "Who are you and why do you want to know?"

"I'm Irma's brother, and I'm anxious to find her after seven years."

"You're Heinz? I've heard a lot about you. I'm Dr. Koenig, a friend of your family. We all knew you'd make it.

"As you know," he went on, "your sister is a devout Catholic and usually goes to late mass on Sunday morning. It will be over in half an hour. Stand in front of that church"—He pointed to the nearest one—"and you'll see both of them coming out."

We exchanged a few more words and went our separate ways. I stood in front of the church and waited. The service ended on schedule, and people came streaming out in their Sunday best. I examined them carefully—it had been a long time since I saw any of my relatives.

Those two walking down the steps side by side had to be Irma and Julius—there was no doubt in my mind. I came up to them and blocked their way. Irma looked affronted, then gaped at me just before she fainted: "Heinz . . ."

Julius caught her before she fell to the pavement. We sat her down on the steps and held our breath while she recovered. Meanwhile, Julius was giving me a joyous reception. Soon enough, Irma recovered and hugged me to no end.

"Hop into our car," she finally told me. "We'll take you to our house on the Arlberg—you'd never find it by yourselves. We're going to fix a big lunch for you—Westphalia ham, potato salad, eggs, Moselle wine, the whole works."

"I'm astonished you're driving a car and have all that good food available, while everyone else is starving around here."

"Don't worry, Heinz, I know a few people," Julius smiled. "You'll be very comfortable with us."

"Sounds good, but I've got my own transportation and will follow you."

I pointed across the street at my white beauty.

"You devil, looks better than my DKW. How did you do it?"

"I'll tell you all about it, dear brother-in-law."

We drove ten minutes out of town to a farmhouse and parked our cars in a large barn.

"We aren't home yet," Julius told me. "We have to walk another ten minutes through the woods. That's where we were hiding from the Gestapo for the last nine months when they were trying to get Irma back in Essen. The farmer here was the only one who knew where we were. He's the one who fed us all these last months. So don't think that every German collaborated with Hitler."

Julius had stayed loyal to his Jewish wife. He had been drafted early in the war, and after the authorities learned he was married to a "non-Aryan," he was put under tremendous pressure to divorce her. His stubborn refusal led to a dishonorable discharge—a dangerous mark to have on your record in Nazi Germany.

The previous September, long after Himmler's goons launched the "Final Solution" in Germany and occupied Europe, Julius had found this backwoods hideout for his family.

We left the woods and approached a simple but solid-looking cabin in a meadow. An excited eleven-year-old boy in *lederhosen* ran out to greet us. It was my nephew Dieter, whom I'd last seen two years earlier in Amsterdam. Irma showed me to my room and started preparing lunch.

"Everything here is yours, Heinz. Stay as long as you want to."

Then Julius approached me with a happy gesture. "We're so glad you survived. Do you think there's any chance that anyone else in the family will come back?"

"Julius, I hate to say it, but the odds are against anyone who was caught in the earlier part of the war. Unfortunately, that includes our parents, and Friedel too. I've heard too many stories about the extermination camps in the east."

"Well, I haven't given up yet. I'll keep hoping until someone can prove that they died. Now let me give you some good news. We tried to provide a playmate for Dieter all through the war, but it seems that the pressure we felt prevented it. As soon as the Allied troops liberated us, Irma became pregnant. She's due around Christmas. Whether it's a boy or a girl, I want to commemorate the event with a name, in any language, that expresses our liberation. We have a few more months to come up with one."

It was hard to find enough food in those days in Germany. It took a lot of contacts and inventive ideas. I approached a butcher in this little town who was in a position to produce a lot of sausage, thanks to all the cattle farmers in the area. The industry was government controlled by then, and rationing was being enforced, but there were always loopholes.

My goal was to secure a good supply for our family, with enough left to trade for other needed goods, like groceries, clothes, and gasoline. Because I was one of the few people in the area with an automobile, we made an arrangement: I would deliver his products at regular intervals to the Ruhr cities; in return he'd supply us with meat we could exchange for other necessities. Money was worthless in those days.

Unfortunately, during one of my first trips, I ran into a captain in the British Military Police, who liked my car very much and found an excuse to confiscate it. All my efforts to get it back failed—he was the law, and he had the last word. When I became too insistent, he threatened to jail me for a few months, and I knew he had the power to do just that. So I gave up, heartbroken. A few weeks later I saw my beauty moving around with letters all over its body: M.P. Well, easy come, easy go. Julius was generous enough to make his DKW available for future trips.

Around that time we remembered that we had to fill our wine cellar for the forthcoming christening of the newborn baby. They had chosen me as godfather, and we decided to invite plenty of friends and go all out by incorporating a celebration of our new freedom.

There was no better place to go looking for wine than the famous Moselle Valley. I packed my vehicle with a good supply of meat to barter. Julius told me the names of a few local wineries and, for my sanity, assigned me a chaperone: a nun named Klara, the real thing, a friend of the family. She had a record of stubborn resistance against the Third Reich and had been deeply involved in Irma's escape from the Gestapo. She wanted to visit one of her relatives near the Moselle, and that was good enough for me.

Luck must have been shining on us both: she, the messenger of God, and I, a non-believer since the Holocaust. You couldn't beat that combination. What a nice odd couple we were.

It was December, and winter had started. The 250 kilometer drive to the south went smoothly, and by early afternoon we were negotiating with the wineries. Within hours our DKW was packed with Moselle. It seems that no one could resist Klara's habit and my sausages.

Our last stop called for a celebration. The farmer's daughter was as appetizing to me as his wine stock. I couldn't resist her offers of various wine tastings during her guided tour of the cellar. It all felt very normal until I hit the fresh air outside. Then the world around me started spinning. A cup of coffee gave me a temporary cure, and I felt sure I'd be able to drive home.

This time we crossed the bridge at Koblenz and joined the Autobahn on the right side, the Rhine side. Darkness had set in, light snow was beginning to fall. The visibility was almost nothing, and too much wine tasting had made me sleepy.

We came to an arrow sign pointing right, obviously requiring us to detour off the Autobahn. I was going at pretty good speed and started turning my wheel with all my strength, pumping the brakes simultaneously. It was too late—the car careened down the embankment. I didn't give up and kept the wheels straight, hoping for the best while Sister Klara whispered some prayers. With a severe jerk, we came to a stop without turning over.

We looked at each other and almost simultaneously asked the same question: "Are you all right?"

Neither of us had a scratch. I stepped out of the car carefully, holding on to the door. It was almost pitch-dark, but I could see well enough to notice a square piece of timber under the front springs, which had prevented us from sliding any farther. Our almost perfectly balanced cargo, the back packed with wine bottles to the roof and the front occupied with two evenly weighted passengers, had worked to our advantage by making the automobile hug the ground. I saw that we had stopped on a gentle slope. Except for those things, I saw nothing.

Klara had left the car by now. She approached me in a calm voice.

"I was praying the whole time on our way down," she said, "and God heard me."

I nodded. I couldn't argue with that one.

We climbed up to the road. Only then did we realize how steep the embankment was. The car showed no signs of damage, but we'd need someone with a strong engine and a long, heavy rope to tow us back up. In the meantime, we walked until we came to a farmhouse.

We pounded on the door till a man woke up and answered. He saw Klara's habit and let us in immediately while we described our predicament.

"Make yourselves comfortable in the living room," he said. "In a few hours, when daylight breaks, I'll arrange a tow for you. By the way, you're in the town of Asbach, where the world-famous 'Asbach Uralt' cognac is distilled."

Once we had settled in, he added: "You overshot the detour on the Autobahn? That makes you a statistic—two autos a week have gone down that embankment. It's a destroyed viaduct, a 100 meter drop. Except you're the first ones to survive. This is the French-occupied zone, and they still hate us for invading them. So they're taking their sweet time letting us rebuild and put up warning signs."

Early the next morning, our host drove up with a heavy Wehrmacht surplus truck equipped with a long, thick rope. When we approached the scene of my "crime," my eyeballs almost popped out.

The decline was long and awesome. Our car had come to a halt in the only place where it flattened out for a few feet like a terrace, one-third of the way down. It took several hours' hard work with primitive equipment to hook up the DKW and pull it back up to the road. The reward of bottles of wine for the participants was well appreciated.

I got behind the wheel and turned the key. The engine started on command.

"It's a miracle," Sister Klara exclaimed.

I was muttering to myself, "Thank you, Auto Union, for building such a rugged car."

On December 18, 1945, Irma gave birth to a healthy, well-formed baby girl. They named her Gabriele, and after long research chose the middle name of Eleuteria, from the ancient Greek word for freedom. Wine flowed like water, and all our friends helped us celebrate the happy event. There was one cloud in the sky—when we looked around at our friends, we remembered who was missing, and we understood without being told that they would never come home again.

My nephew, Dieter, was a sheer delight. He followed me like a shadow, and a wonderful camaraderie developed between us. He was a sharp kid and caught on quickly to all situations. When he was twelve, I let him take the wheel of the car sometimes during our frequent trips together. I knew we had a very promising young man on our hands.

I was happy to be with my family and was living better than most people in Germany at the time. I had good food, decent clothes, a car at my disposal, and beautiful girls to choose from. I even got involved in politics. My friends and relatives started dropping remarks, which all amounted to the unspoken question:

"Well, Heinz, now that you're back home and doing well, when are you going to start your own family?"

I had to disappoint them all—I was still too much of a rebel to live like that, I mean, like a bourgeois. I was also eager to learn whether any of my friends had survived the war and returned to Amsterdam or Paris.

At that point, the enormity of the destruction and the suffering of its victims was having a powerful impact on me. Only a handful of people, of all the millions who had been swept up by the transports for the "crime" of having more than two Jewish grandparents, had returned from the Holocaust. Their reports were horrifying, and far worse than what I had experienced.

They would talk about the terrible train journeys in packed cattle cars to Auschwitz, during which so many died. About the station platform, where an SS officer would point his thumb up or down—almost always down. The latter meant immediate consignment to the gas chambers, then the crematoriums, which burned day and night. Only a handful of strong young men, a few pretty women, and some with specific skills—doctors, nurses, architects—were allowed to live a little longer.

Still shuddering, they would talk about the sadistic games the SS guards played—taking babies from their mothers' arms and throwing them high in the air for target practice.

And if you survived the selection on the station platform, it wasn't likely to be for long. You would be starved to death, or be worked to death, or be tortured with medical experiments until you were "reclassified" for the gas chambers.

A few survivors I knew had been lucky enough to be sent to Theresienstadt, the Nazis' "model" camp, the one they allowed the Red Cross to inspect.

The toll among the Resistance fighters was also quite heavy. Many had been betrayed by their neighbors to the Gestapo in return for money, food, or a chance to save their own skins. I guess some people just couldn't bear the war any longer. The most tragic story I heard was about one of our most committed leaders, a man who had saved hundreds of lives and had just received the Croix de Guerre for his service to France. He was walking on the roadside near his village, just out for a morning stroll, when an Allied military vehicle passed too close. The passenger door disengaged from its lock and struck him, killing him instantly.

Now came the moment of truth: I returned to Amsterdam.

I still thought of Gisela constantly. She would be about twenty years old now, and I had already heard that the Gestapo hadn't swept her up, because her mother was "Aryan." She was living in the same place, so one evening I just knocked on her door, to surprise her. When she answered, her beautiful brown eyes rolled back and she was speechless for what seemed like an eternity. Then she hugged and kissed me to death.

(left to right) Gisela sister Gury, Henry Goldsmith, Gisela Samuel

"The war's been over for a year," she told me. "I wasn't able to get any reliable information about you. I'm so happy you're alive."

"Gisela, I've been living in Germany. I couldn't bring myself to get involved in any deep relationship. You're the last one I wanted to hurt. But I'm here now."

Now she looked guilty. "I have a confession, too. I was waiting for you until two months ago. Then I got confused—I couldn't be sure if the rumors were true that you'd survived or whether you'd changed your heart. Then I met a soldier from the Jewish Brigade of Palestine, who'd seen some heavy combat in Italy and had given up all hope for his future. But I was able to comfort him, and I had this yearning to contribute to Palestine for the sake of my ancestors. Now we're engaged, and I'm going there with him."

"That's noble of you, Gisela. What more can I say?"

She kissed me again. "I knew you'd understand, Heinz. Don't look so sad. Let's enjoy a last few days together."

My cousins, Hannes and Berta, insisted that I live with them while in Amsterdam. They made up a room for me and fed me well. Another pleasant surprise was that my three closest friends, Ludwig, Fred, and Leo, had all survived the war, too. We celebrated our reunion with a trip to Paris.

Things weren't too good there either. Few deportees had returned from the camps, many Resistance fighters had been killed, and the country was still recovering from the war, its economy in shambles. We met a few friends, enjoyed the pleasures of the city, and returned to Amsterdam after a few days.

Ludwig, the most straight-laced of us, happily took a job in his brother-in-law's leather-goods factory. The rest of us weren't ready to settle down. We decided we needed a good set of wheels, and where better to look than in Germany?

We set out immediately. I knew the market there and had strong contacts, so we bought some goods in Holland that we could sell at a high markup—high enough to buy a good used car.

Out of old habit, we prepared our travel documents ourselves and boarded the British military train in French uniforms, leaving from London. We arrived on the continent at Hoek van Holland and continued by way of Utrecht to the Ruhr, which was in the British occupation zone. Our smuggled merchandise was packed in standard suitcases, and there wasn't any border check. Nothing on this trip made our hearts beat faster, unlike during the war, when I always had to travel under Nazi surveillance.

My cousin Berta had received some information that her sister Frieda had been seen at the Lublinka concentration camp, and she wanted to explore this possibility of hope. My part in this would be to look up a family in the city of Mülheim an der Ruhr, whose son had shared her fate. Leo Baldeschwiler was his name, and they would be listed in the telephone directory.

This mission for Berta ranked high on my list. Little did I know that it would change my own life drastically.

16
GOODBYE EUROPE

WE LEFT THE train at Oberhausen and looked up a business contact I had made there. He was a jack-of-all-trades, well trusted in his community as well as by me. He seemed very interested in handling the entire transaction for us, so we decided to let him try.

Within twenty-four hours he had sold all our goods for us and presented us with a Ford V8 convertible in mint condition. All three of us loved it, and went to work on it immediately, preparing it for the border inspections. Our business friend found us some craftsmen to paint military emblems all over the body. We also changed the license plate, synchronizing it with our old French Resistance unit. By now that unit had become part of the French Armed Forces, so we applied the letters FFI (Forces Française Interieur) all over the car.

We were in seventh heaven and had an urge to show off our new possession to everyone we knew and have the time of our lives while we were at it. First, though, I had to contact this family with the strange name of Baldeschwiler. We got directions to Mülheim and soon found ourselves in front of a neat, simple house with a good-sized garden in a suburb of the city. I approached the front door with hesitation and rang the bell.

A pretty girl in her teens opened and gave us a bewildered look. "What can I do for you?"

"May I speak to your mother, please?"

"She isn't home. You'll have to deal with me."

"Well, would you let us in, please? It's important. Our names are Heinz, Leo, and Fred. We're living in Holland now. We'd like some information about your brother."

Sadness cast a shadow on her face. She stared for a moment, and then let us in.

"My name is Ellen," she said. "My mother is out for the afternoon and will return soon. We're the only survivors in our family."

She told us she was working as a milliner's apprentice (this was her afternoon off), that she helped her mother with cooking and cleaning, that she waited in long lines to buy rationed food, and that she sometimes rode on packed trains looking for food, coming home with sacks of potatoes she'd bought from local farmers. All three of us were impressed with her outspoken manner. She was sixteen, but the war had aged her quickly. After hearing about the hardships she'd suffered, we wanted to show her a good time during our stay in Germany.

She was the child of a mixed marriage, her father Catholic and her mother Jewish. Her brother had been deported to a concentration camp in Poland early in the war and never returned. Her mother had been picked up by the Gestapo nine months before the war ended. By then, the Nazi war machine was so short of laborers that instead of being gassed in one of the camps, she had been sent to a labor camp in Berlin. Her task was altering military uniforms, in return for which she received fair treatment and some food. She survived, and returned home to find her daughter all alone, with shrapnel wound in her chest, which fortunately healed. Her father and young man a friend of the family had been standing next to her in the backyard, listening to the artillery as the desperately awaited Americans encircled the Ruhr. They weren't as lucky as Ellen—both were killed instantly by an exploding shell.

Mrs. Baldeschwiler, a stocky woman in her early fifties, finally came home. She was surprised to see three strange men in her living room, but after I explained our mission, she told us all she could and even invited us to stay for dinner.

The following night, we parked our car in front of the department store where Ellen worked. Once her shift ended, she left the building with a group of her coworkers, who stared with amazement and jealousy while we whisked her away.

It was an eventful evening. We went to the opera, then went looking for more excitement. I remembered my sister telling me about a fanatic Nazi neighbor who always used to stop her from entering the air raid shelter during Allied bombing raids.

"There's no room for non-Aryans," he exclaimed. "Stay out there with your friends, the air pirates."

I was in just the mood for him that night, and figured he'd be home by now. A short ride to Essen West brought us to a deserted neighborhood. We took our wristwatches off and handed them to Ellen, who remained in the car. Then Leo removed his "Luger" from the glove compartment and stuck it in his belt under his jacket. We walked up one flight and knocked at the door. A man in his late thirties opened up. Seeing the three of us, he tried to slam the door shut. But I was faster and blocked it with my foot, knowing that Leo was behind me and covering me.

"Is your name Schreck?" I demanded.

He nodded yes.

"In that case, I owe you one. Do you remember your neighbor, Mrs. Spitmann?"

"Oh yes, we were very good neighbors."

"If that's so, how come you always gave her such a hard time and banned her from the air-raid shelter?"

"Oh no, that isn't true, I always treated her like an equal, even if she *was* Jewish."

Liar. I could see it in his face. I glanced at his hall closet and saw his brown SA uniform still hanging there. Then my blood really started to boil. I shoved him across the room and started pounding his head against the wall. He freed himself, reached into the closet, and brought out a short piece of iron pipe. He started swinging it and missed me by a hair. A moment later, I heard a click behind me and saw my opponent freeze and turn pale.

Leo had cocked his gun and was pointing it at him. I jerked the pipe out of his hands, relieved Leo of his weapon, and handed him a bonus:

"He's all yours, Leo."

Leo went at him as if he was letting out all his frustration from the entire war. I stopped him when the screams of a woman in the house became unbearable.

When we got back to the car, we saw that all the windows around us were occupied with people staring in awe at our vehicle. We took off right away—I had no intention of taking on the whole neighborhood. Then I turned to Ellen: "Since we're all having so much fun, what else would you like for excitement tonight?"

She thought for a moment. "Come to think, my girlfriend Ruth is having a birthday party tonight. I don't think she'd mind if you guys crashed it."

So it was. We raced back to Mülheim and found ourselves welcome at a lively party. We telephoned Ellen's mother to apologize for her daughter's delayed return, promising she would be safe with us. It was almost dawn when we delivered Ellen home safe and sound.

A few days later, we were on our way back to Amsterdam, the proud owners of a beautiful convertible. I was driving. The border crossing went smoothly, but by then a shadow was falling on our friendship: all three of us had fallen in love with the same girl.

We tried to be realistic and set our sudden rivalry to one side. More adventure was calling. We felt secure crossing borders in this vehicle with our documents. Our next trip was to Brussels, where we combined pleasure with a little black marketeering. It all went well, and we were having a good time until we were driving back to Holland again.

A few miles south of the border, we were stopped by two British military police. They were the same goons, by type anyway, as had confiscated my car in Germany the year before. It was our bad luck to have been intercepted by the military police commander of Belgium, a fanatic former Scotland Yard inspector with no sense of humor. It wasn't enough for him to take our car away—he also arrested us and delivered us to the stockade in Brussels.

The discovery of a handgun almost had him frothing at the mouth. He immediately accused us of being members of the Haganah, a Jewish resistance organization that by then was fighting the British in Palestine, helping found the State of Israel and smuggling Jewish refugees to their new homeland from all over Europe. It took three grueling months for us to convince our jailers we were harmless.

We returned to Amsterdam, broke and humiliated, and started looking for ways to settle down. I found a job with an electrical contractor and attended night school a few times a week, studying radio technology. There was no shortage of girls in the city. An evening on the dance floor was usually enough for me. I wasn't the only one chasing to catch up with good times, now that the war had ended.

I soon found out that both my friends, same as me, were in correspondence with Ellen. I'd have to move quickly. Her letters back to me weren't exactly encouraging, so I left for Germany to see for myself what her hopes might be.

Like all mothers, Mrs. Baldeschwiler was highly protective of her daughter and planning to find the best possible husband for her. She assigned me a room and took me in as a boarder. I looked into the possibility of obtaining a tobacco wholesale and retail license, since my family had done well in that business before the war. I succeeded, and was allotted a certain quantity of goods, which were always sold out before the day ended. It took a lot of contacts to get enough merchandise.

Meanwhile, my brother-in-law Julius had built up a lucrative business in Westphalia and needed a larger vehicle. I bought his DKW from him and became mobile. I spent most of my time visiting distributors and factories, pulling cigars, cigarettes, and tobacco out of their teeth. Finally, I started making good money, and Mrs. Baldeschwiler started seeing me as a serious candidate.

On Ellen's eighteenth birthday, January 20, 1948, we got engaged. Now I had to prove that I could support a family. I managed to arrange some tobacco concessions at nearby racetracks. That meant I could sell my merchandise at higher prices than in a retail store.

Inflation was soaring, and most of the goods I traded could only be found on the black market. Then suddenly the bubble burst: we got up one morning and heard on the radio that all the money we were holding was worthless—it would have to be traded with proper identification at a local bank against a new currency. The ratio was 10:1. For every ten Reichsmark, the eligible trader would receive one new Deutschemark.

For the next few weeks, everyone was broke; and this had to happen just before our scheduled wedding in July. The advantages, of course, were immense. All the shop owners were eager to sell their merchandise, and everyone was bending over backwards to offer their services. Meanwhile, construction was booming, with houses and factories rising from the ashes at lightning speed. Everyone wanted to lay their hands on that new, good-looking

Ellen and Henry Goldsmith wedding photo 1948

money, but most people were having to start from scratch. This was the beginning of the *Wirtschaftswunder*, the "business miracle," that was going to make Germany an economic powerhouse within a few years.

But that was in the future. Meanwhile, we scraped together enough for a modest wedding attended by a small circle of friends and a handful of family survivors. Our honeymoon would have to wait a few more months, until we were financially sound again. We accomplished that in January 1949, when we joined a winter sports group for a week in the Alps, a stone's throw from Hitler's retreat in Berchtesgaden. The SS barracks that guarded it had been bombed to rubble by the Allies, but the "Almighty's" Alpine lodge on the Berghof had been left intact and was attracting hordes of visitors.

But this was our week. Hitler and his thugs had been crushed. We had come here to gaze at the mountains, learn how to ski, and enjoy our youth and each other. We hiked for hours high into the mountains, then tried to slide down again on these on these strange, long boards, without much success. It was far more difficult than it looked. I was also concerned that Ellen, at the young age of nineteen, was tiring so easily. Our landlady, an experienced woman in her forties, came up with the answer. She told Ellen one evening:

"My child, I've been watching you for a few days and listening to your complaints about being tired and nauseous. I think you're pregnant."

On October 13, 1949, we were blessed with a healthy boy weighing nine pounds. We named him Frank and gave him the middle name Alfred, in memory of my father. Nine days later, he consumed his first booze when they stuck a piece of cotton soaked with brandy in his mouth. That was supposed to knock him out while he had his foreskin cut off.

Franky was a big baby, which had made for a difficult labor. But mother and son finally came home. Franky made wonderful progress, and with a new member of our family to consider, our thoughts vaulted into the future. Europe was no place for a young family in those days. History was telling us that all we had seen could happen again.

We weren't willing to take any chances. I thought about all the Americans I had met. We were young, strong, and ambitious, as well as confident that we could build a good life in a new country.

I contacted the U.S. Consulate and learned that to immigrate to his country we would need an affidavit from an American citizen. We had already tried that, approaching relatives and acquaintances in the States. No one was willing to take financial responsibility for a family of three.

There had to be another way. I looked hard into it, and learned that the status of displaced persons (DPs) had recently been changed. As a Holocaust survivor, I was eligible for that category, even though I was living in Germany again.

My application was answered soon. After a preliminary interview, the three of us were sent to the DP processing center in Wentorf near Hamburg. We were in with a few thousand other prospective immigrants, housed in twenty huge barracks that had once been occupied by the German military.

Our quarters were primitive, and the sanitary conditions were the same, especially with a three-month-old baby to care for. The medical exam was very intense, and so was all the bureaucratic red tape. The process took eight weeks, with long interruptions that did nothing to lift our spirits.

On the bright side, we were shown documentaries and attended lectures that told us about our new home, and we were able to take English-language classes. Finally, the great day arrived—we were transferred to the embarkment center near Bremen.

We had heard about the liberty ships, which were packed with newcomers like ourselves to cross the Atlantic. A special bonus, though, was waiting for us. Thanks to Franky, who was only five months old now, we were eligible to make this trip by air. The anticipation of our first flight and the beginning of my second life in the land of unlimited opportunities was immense.

Frank, Cynthia, Alex, Garrett Goldsmith

Henry Goldsmith's TV repair shop Aspen, Colorado

Good-bye, Europe. I leave you with mixed emotions.

Ellen and Henry Goldsmith, Cynthia and Frank Goldsmith, and
brother Steven Goldsmith in Aspen in the 90's

Frank and Steve Goldsmith

The Goldsmith family in Aspen, Colorado

(Left to right) Henry, Cynthia, Alex, Frank and Ellen